Keys to Interpreting the Bible

KEYS TO INTERPRETING THE BIBLE

Earl P. McQuay

BROADMAN PRESS
NASHVILLE, TENNESSEE

© Copyright 1993 • Broadman Press
All rights reserved
4281-58
ISBN: 0-8054-8158-3
Dewey Decimal Classification: 220.07
Subject Heading: Bible. STUDY
Library of Congress Catalog Card Number: 92-6334
Printed in the United States of America

Library of Congress Cataloging-in-Publication Data
McQuay, Earl P.
    Keys to interpreting the Bible / Earl P. McQuay
        p.   cm.
    ISBN 0-8054-8158-3
    1. Bible—Hermeneutics.   I. Title.
BS476.M3483   1993
220.6'01—dc20   92-6334
                                                                             CIP

Dedication

To Helen,
my dear sister
and lifelong friend.

Contents

Part I
Introduction

The royal traveler was reading from the marvelous fifty-third chapter of Isaiah when Philip asked him, "Do you understand what you are reading?" The Ethiopian eunuch wanted to understand. He had made a spiritual pilgrimage to Jerusalem to worship and now had stopped in the desert to read the Scriptures. His reply to Philip, however, was "How could I, unless someone guides me?" (Acts 8:30, 31).

God has spoken to us in His Word in language that is clear. His Word can be explained accurately. The proper interpretation of the Bible is the privilege and responsibility of every Christian. God encourages us to study His Word, promising that He will enable us to understand it and apply it in our lives.

Today, there is an increased interest in theological hermeneutics (the science and methodology of interpretation of the Scriptures). This book simplifies hermeneutics. It outlines the basic principles that enable a person to interpret the Scriptures with confidence.

Part I introduces you to you—the student and interpreter of the Bible—and to significant historical information about other interpreters of the Bible. Part II covers general "laws" related to literal interpretation, author's intention, historical setting, purpose and plan, word meaning, grammar, context, and related Scripture. Part III includes special principles for interpreting special kinds of literary form: figures of speech, symbol, type, parable and allegory, Hebrew poetry, prophecy, and doctrinal problems.

Here is a set of "keys" that will enable you to open the Word of God to your understanding and life application.

1.
Do I Read You Well?

A character in *Alice in Wonderland* said, "A word means precisely what I want it to mean—nothing more and nothing less." For you to treat biblical words in this way would be tragic. In studying the Scriptures, you must know how to determine what God actually is saying and what it means to you, not merely what you want it to mean.

The interpretation of Scripture can be a fascinating and rewarding experience. The proper interpretation of the Bible is the privilege and responsibility not only of pastors and theologians but every Christian. God's Word calls upon every believer to read and understand its message and to apply its truth to every area of life. One does not have to be a scholar to learn to interpret the Bible intelligently. After all, the Bible was written to meet the spiritual needs of the common man and woman.

To be regenerated by the Holy Spirit is the foundational prerequisite for being a Bible student. Without the new birth experience, one cannot begin to understand God's Word. Only a spiritually reborn person is able to comprehend spiritual truth:

> Jesus answered and said to him, "Truly, truly, I say to you, unless one is born again, he cannot see the kingdom of God" (John 3:3).

> But a natural man does not accept the things of the Spirit of God; for they are foolishness to him, and he cannot understand

them, because they are spiritually appraised. But he who is spiritual appraises all things, yet he himself is appraised by no man (1 Cor. 2:14-15).

Besides regeneration, there are three vital needs for the Bible student. Based on the following Scriptures, can you identify three needs that begin with the letter *D*?

(1) The Bible student must have a D _____ for the truth of God;

Blessed are they which do hunger and thirst after righteousness: for they shall be filled (Matt. 5:6, KJV).

Draw nigh to God, and he will draw nigh to you (Jas. 4:8, KJV).

(2) The Bible student must have a D _____ upon the Holy Spirit:

For to us God revealed them through the Spirit; for the Spirit searches all things, even the depths of God. . . . which things we speak, not in words taught by human wisdom, but in those taught also by the Spirit, combining spiritual thoughts with spiritual words (1 Cor. 2:10, 13).

But when He, the Spirit of truth, comes, He will guide you into all the truth; for He will not speak on His own initiative, but whatever He hears, He will speak; and He will disclose to you what is to come (John 16:13).

(3) The Bible student must have a D _____ in applying himself to the study of God's word:

You search the Scriptures, because you think that in them you have eternal life; and it is these that bear witness of Me (John 5:39).

Be diligent to present yourself approved to God as a workman who does not need to be ashamed, handling accurately the word of truth (2 Tim. 2:15).

The Word of God is presented in human language that can be understood when interpreted according to the laws of human language. The Bible itself gives guidance for developing a system of interpretation that is true to both Scripture and reason. Every Christian can profit by a careful look at the principles for interpreting Scripture that are in harmony with the Bible itself. The teachings of the Bible will be clear to the person who treats the Scriptures honestly and intelligently.

Almost all religious disputes and dissensions since the Bible was written have been related to the question of how to interpret the Bible. Peter spoke of the self-destruction of those who hastily adopted distorted views of the Scriptures instead of seeking the Holy Spirit's leading in interpretation. He referred to their treatment of Paul's Letters "which the untaught and unstable distort, as they do also the rest of the Scriptures, to their own destruction" (2 Pet. 3:16).

Do I read you well? should be our concern as we look into the Bible. In the following pages we will outline some principles that will enable you to interpret the Scriptures with confidence. A grasp of these principles will enable you to pray, "I read you loudly and clearly."

To whet your appetite for Bible study, look up the following Scripture verses that reveal the value of Bible study, and fill in the blanks.

A. *The Bible is* described in 2 Timothy 3:15-17 (KJV) as:
   1. A _____ - Centered Book
   2. A _____ - Saving Book
   3. A _____ - Inspired Book
   4. A _____ - Perfecting Book

B. The *value* of studying the Bible is understood when one comprehends the purposes that the Word of God fulfills in the human life. A number of figures of speech are used in the Word to illustrate its significance. Look up each of the following verses and note the imagery used and the personal application.
   1. James 1:23-25 - The Bible is a *mirror* that *convicts* me of sin, reveals my true condition, and shows me what change is needed.

2. Jeremiah 23:29 -

3. Ephesians 5:26 -

4. Deuteronomy 8:3, Psalm
   19:10; Hebrews 5:12, 14 -

5. Psalm 119:105 -

6. Ephesians 6:16-17 -

7. Psalm 119:72 -

8. Luke 8:5, 11 -

Check your answers with the Answer List in the back of
the book.

2.
Historical Schools of Biblical Interpretation

In the course of Christian history, many methods have been employed in interpreting the Scriptures. Following is a historical sketch of hermeneutics, the methodology of interpretaon. In the introduction to his survey of hermeneutics, Berkeley Mickelsen insisted that we may profit from a review of the history of interpretation:

> Interpretation is not something new. Throughout the ages men have used certain principles with which to interpret the Scriptures. Many excellent books have been written about the history of interpretation. . . . lessons can be drawn from the procedures of the past . . . history shows that erroneous principles have often spoiled the exegetical work of fine men, some of whom were great saints. This should be a warning to us against carelessness in interpretation. There is less excuse for us because we can profit by the lessons of the past. It should also remind us that the use of correct procedures must be founded upon a dedication to God, a consecration to the task, and a love for men which unites all that we are and know.[1]

Jewish Interpretation

The first interpreters of Scripture appear to be the "scribes" who arose in Ezra's day. These could speak truth (as in Neh. 8:8) or could write falsehood (Jer. 8:8). The scribes of Ezra's day were dedicated to the truth. We are told that they "explained the law to the people while the people remained in their place. And they read from the book, from the law of God, translating [marg.: explaining] to give the sense so that they understood the reading" (Neh. 8:7-8). The scribes expounded the Scriptures in order that the people might understand their meaning.

Apparently, the scribes continued as a group of men in Israel who copied the sacred writings and gave to the common people a translation and interpretation of the Scriptures. As these men turned away from the truth of God in their hearts, it showed in their interpretations of Scripture. Jesus condemned the scribes of His day as hypocrites who misguided the people (Matt. 23).

Some Jews withdrew to ascetic communities such as Qumran to try to live in conformity to the law of God. They copied the Scriptures and wrote commentaries. Usually, the biblical material was explained in terms of the community and eschatology. In an effort to apply the Scriptures to themselves and their own times, they neglected a basic principle of sound interpretation of Scripture—to find out what the author intended to convey.

Rabbis of Israel, between 168 B.C. and A.D. 10, kept alive biblical interpretation through debates. They erred, however, by looking for "deeper hidden meanings" rather than clarifying the precise meaning conveyed by the language. From A.D. 10 to A.D. 550, the Jewish *Midrashim* and *Mishna* commentaries on Scripture stressed the practical (*what* God demands and *how* persons should respond to Him) with speculative imagination present on almost every page. In the rabbinic literature, we see how far afield interpreters can stray when they fail to base their interpretations upon the historical context of a passage.

Hellenistic Jews were those scattered throughout the Mediterranean world who adopted the Greek language as their own. In Alexandria they produced the Septuagint, the Greek translation of the Scriptures (250-150 B.C.). Their method of interpretation was often allegorical. Rather than considering what the original writer was trying to say (the grammatical-historical meaning), they treated what they wanted to say as the only important factor. The allegorical method views the apparent, surface sense of a writing as paralleling and illustrating a deeper spiritual sense. Philo of Alexandria made allegory his principal method.

Early Church Fathers

Within the church, the allegorizing method grew until it had a firm hold on biblical studies. Howbeit, there were some careful exegetical studies on major questions that enabled the church to establish an orthodox view of the deity and humanity of Christ and the relationship of the three Persons of the Trinity.

The Alexandrian group of scholars resorted to allegorizing. Though the school of Antioch emphasized historical interpretation, it lost influence; and the Alexandrian school of allegorizing became predominate.

Clement of Alexandria built upon the allegorical method of Philo. Clement was the first to justify and explain the meaning of the allegorical method. He taught that all Scripture speaks in a mysterious language of symbols. Every word and syllable of Scripture has its meaning, which usually is not the obvious one. The meaning must be interpreted by one who is devoted to the church and who has faith in Christ.

Due to conflict regarding the method of interpretation, writers sensed a need of an external authority that would permanently fix the meaning of Scripture. This authority was found in the Church, where the Scriptures had been preserved by those who stood in the apostolic succession. Irenaeus and Tertullian insisted upon the authority of the church in matters of interpretation. Irenaeus urged conformity with the church at Rome where, he pointed out, apostolic tradition had been faithfully preserved. Tertullian is best remembered for his polemical writings which are careful defenses of the Christian faith.

The most distinguished member of the Alexandrian school was Origen, who taught that exegesis of Scripture must result from prayer for guidance from God, and from diligent work aimed at discovering the figures hidden behind every verse, word, and syllable of Scripture. Origen taught, for example, that Rebekah's drawing water for Abraham's servant and his cattle meant that we must come to the wells of Scripture in order to meet Christ.

Augustine transposed the insights of Irenaeus and Tertullian, both of whom indulged in allegory, into a higher key. He insisted on the need for learning and on the ultimate authority in interpretation as the Scripture itself. Yet at the same time he was deeply devoted to the authority of the church. He believed that the truth had been handed down in the tradition of the church. Though Augustine and Jerome taught that sound principles are important for interpretation, they also continued to practice the method of allegorization. Allegorization took over the methodology of biblical scholars for a thousand years.

Middle Ages

Allegory had a hold on the minds of medieval theologians. Interpreters were led far astray from literal, historical, and contextual meanings. Collections of allegorical interpretations showed, for example, that the word *sea* could mean a gathering of water, Scripture, the present age, the human heart, the active life, heathen, or baptism.[2]

The church fathers and the monks distinguished between the literal and the spiritual meaning, which they believed was required by the Scriptural declaration, "The letter kills, but the Spirit gives life" (2 Cor. 3:6). In his book, Kenneth Hagen has explained the popular fourfold sense of interpretation:

> The most famous form of the multi-level approach became the
> *quadriga*, the fourfold sense: the literal tells what happened
> (historical sense), the allegorical teaches what is to be believed,

the tropological or moral what is to be done, and the analogical where it is going or "tending." The usual example was Jerusalem, which refers literally to the city, allegorically to the church, tropologically to the soul, and analogically to heaven. The monks put this to rhyme. The point is that the letter is a mirror of the almost limitless depth of meaning.[3]

Though Thomas Aquinas represented a trend in the right direction with his stress upon literal interpretation, he also was involved in much allegorical interpretation. The reformation began when men questioned the allegorical or mystical approach to Scripture.

Reformation and Post-Reformation Periods

Through his own independent study of Scripture, Martin Luther became discontented with the traditionalism and allegorizing in the church of Rome. He abandoned the fourfold interpretation of the medieval period. His new emphasis on the single fundamental meaning led to a greater clarity of Scripture. He asserted the right of each believer to interpret the Bible for himself under the illumination of the Holy Spirit. With a biblical interpretation that was centered in Christ, Luther underscored the main themes of the gospel and balanced the literal or grammatical sense with the spiritual depth of meaning.

John Calvin was the outstanding biblical interpreter and theologian of the Reformation. He interpreted the Scriptures grammatically and historically. He brought together the Spirit's work in inspiration with the Spirit's illumination of the interpreter.

In the two centuries following Luther and Calvin, a great variety of views appeared, many based upon reason, systems, and abstract formulations as the final authority. Some, like Pascal, opposed rationalism and emphasized careful, humble study of the Scriptures to find God.

Nineteenth Century

Historical criticism developed in the nineteenth century and was largely controlled by a framework of naturalistic and philosophical assumptions. Higher critics demanded that every belief be submitted to critical questioning, and nothing be accepted simply on the basis of tradition. The authorship, date, occasion, and purpose of the biblical writings came under critical examination. The method of "textual criticism" was to evaluate the manuscripts themselves. Some insisted that Moses could not have written the whole of the five books of the Pentateuch. Biblical criticism argued for a purely historical, nondoctrinal, approach to the Bible. Attempts were made to identify different theological outlooks within the Bible itself. Comparisons of biblical faith with the background of other cults and religions were made, with the assertion of possible borrowings from them.

Some who renounced the arbitrariness of rationalism, but who joined in the careful weighing of historical evidence, produced exegetical commentaries of abiding value. The Bible student will recognize the names of the following who wrote monumental commentaries: Alford, Broadus, Delitzsch, Ellicott, Hort, Hodge, Keil, Lightfoot, Westcott, and Zahn. They treated the critical problems of grammar, lexicography, and historical background with respect to the Spirit's inspired message in marked contrast to the rationalistic interpreters.

Twentieth Century

In the first half of the twentieth century, apparently under the pressure of the newer trends of German scholars in higher criticism, commentators generally gave more attention to backgrounds than to the spiritual message of the Scriptures. Some scholars continued their "quest for the historical Jesus," but the unveiled Jesus usually turned out to be an ethical teacher without deity, miracles, or saving power. Other scholars abandoned interest in the historical Jesus altogether, preferring to demythologize the Gospels. In striking contrast, Evangelicals have experienced theological renewal since World War II, and have produced a number of commentaries that deal more with the message of the Bible than with how it came to be written.

Conclusion

A study of the historical schools of biblical interpretation may teach us to be careful to avoid allegorization, mystical speculation, and spiritualization in our hermeneutics. Our task is to expound the Scriptures with a proper view of its grammatical-historical context that we may understand the author's intended meaning. We must seek to understand correctly what a passage *says* and what it *means* in application to our lives today.

Hagen summarized the present hermeneutical task of evangelicals as follows:

> Evangelicals have always made a "high" view of biblical authority a basic tenet of their faith. In spite of the widespread debate today over the exact formulation of such issues as "inerrancy," evangelicals consistently stress that Scripture alone must dictate our faith. While there is cognizance of the complex nature of the interpretive task and the factor of preunderstanding as shaping that interpretation, there is unanimity that the intention of the author is both a possible goal and a necessary element in determining the meaning of the Bible in our day. At the same time, the relevant significance of Scripture is also stressed, and the interdependence between exegesis, biblical theology, historical theology, systematic theology, and contextualization forms the core of evangelical hermeneutics.
>
> The grammatical-historical method predominates. The tools of textual and source criticism, syntactical (grammar) and semantic (word) study, and form, redaction, and narrative criticisms, are all subordinate to the task of elucidating the text.[4]

Part II
Master Keys:
General Hermeneutics

There is a science that is undoubtedly the most important of all in today's explosion of scientific knowledge. It is the science of biblical hermeneutics. *Hermeneutics* is the term used to designate the science of interpretation. The word is derived from the Greek verb *hermēneuō*, which means "to interpret or explain." Biblical hermeneutics is the science of interpreting the Bible.

Paul exhorted young Timothy to exercise great care in handling the Scriptures: "Be diligent to present yourself approved to God as a workman who does not need to be ashamed, handling accurately the word of truth" (2 Tim. 2:15). To handle "accurately" the Word of God demands sound principles of interpretation. Your task as a Bible interpreter is to disclose the original meaning of a Bible statement, that is, the meaning the Bible writer had in mind.

Some principles of interpretation apply to all portions of the Bible and must be followed every time one interprets the Scriptures. These principles are grouped under the category of "general hermeneutics." General hermeneutics involves the general "laws" that guide us in interpreting all kinds of language. Principles related to general hermeneutics are found in the first eight keys.

"Special hermeneutics" covers added principles for interpreting special kinds of literary forms such as Hebrew poetry, prophecy, types, and parables. Principles related to special hermeneutics are covered in the last seven keys.

Let's first consider eight general hermeneutical principles. These relate to literal interpretation, author's intention, historical setting, purpose and plan, word meaning, grammar, context, and related Scripture.

3.
Literal Interpretation

 Interpret the Bible Literally

To interpret the Bible literally is to interpret its words and sentences according to their natural, normal, and usual sense. Ramm defines the literal meaning as *"the customary, socially-acknowledged designation of a word."*[5] The literal meaning of a passage is the precise meaning of the language of the author according to the laws of grammar.

Failing to take a passage literally can result in all sorts of fanciful interpretations. Your approach to Bible interpretation should be similar to your approach to interpreting the current newspaper, that is, to seek to understand the words in their plain and usual sense. "Spiritualizing" is a danger that results from failing to follow a consistently literal interpretation of the Bible. Spiritualizing strains to find hidden spiritual meanings that are not clearly indicated by the writer and are not consistent with the plain, ordinary use of language. God has not given us His revelation in confusing language that allows people to read into the Bible their own meanings.

Any passage should be interpreted literally unless the literal sense makes no sense. An oft-quoted, helpful guideline is: "If the literal sense makes good sense, seek no other sense, lest it result in nonsense." For example, it makes sense to interpret Isaiah 11:6 literally. "The wolf will dwell with the lamb" indicates that even the animals will be at peace with one another when Jesus establishes His kingdom on earth. On the other hand, common sense and a study of the context indicates that Jesus' discussion of separating the sheep from the goats in Matthew 25:32-33 is a reference to human beings, the saved and the unsaved.

Even a figure of speech has a literal interpretation. The literal meaning of a figure is the intended meaning of the imagery employed. The literal meaning is the proper meaning as determined by the social usage and understanding of the figure as it is used in its context.

Try Key #1

Read Philippians 3:1-14, and then read the following two interpretations of this passage:

A. The Jewish nation traditionally has adhered to the ceremonial and moral laws of God in the Torah. Yet the Jews zealously have resisted and persecuted the church of Christ; therefore, they have failed to experience the true righteousness of God; but when the Lord returns to earth, Israel will die to her old beliefs of salvation through fleshly means, turn from her past rejection of the Messiah, and lay hold upon Christ as her Lord. Then Israel will be in a position to fulfill the goal originally designed for her by God.

B. Paul was a zealous follower of Jewish law as the means of salvation until he became converted to Jesus Christ. Things that he considered most valuable in the old unregenerate life, he now counts as worthless. His goal in life now is to know Christ as his Lord and to fulfill Christ's purpose in his life.

1. Which of the above interpretations is the literal interpretation? _____

2. Which of the above interpretations involves spiritualization? _____

Check your answers with the Answer List in the back of the book.

4.
Author's Intention

 Interpret a Passage According to the Author's Single Intended Meaning.

The Bible is a human communication and is understandable when interpreted according to the principles of human communication. The laws of normal human language are a part of our creation in the image of God. When one seeks to communicate, one's true intent in speech is to convey thought, and one views language as a reliable medium of communication.

In human language, a statement must be considered to have one basic meaning. When a person speaks, he or she intends for the words to convey one idea. The speaker does not intend for each statement to be interpreted in several different ways. The hearer, therefore, must understand the single intended meaning. Unless the author says there is a second intended meaning, the statement made must be taken as having only one meaning. Even an idiom, symbol, figure of speech, poetry, or prophecy conveys only one idea at a time. If the meaning of a word changes when used elsewhere, the context and sentence structure will determine the variant meaning. Ordinarily there can be only one true meaning. Only when a second meaning is given to a biblical statement by the Lord Jesus or the Holy Spirit through a subsequent biblical writer should it be accepted with equal authority as the initial, plain meaning of a passage.

Even when a figure of speech is used, it conveys only one idea. To understand what that idea is, you must determine what the language meant when the author used it. Work hard to grasp the intended meaning of the author.

The most obvious meaning usually is the correct meaning.

The usual and most natural sense of a word or passage should be considered correct unless the context demands otherwise. When a word or passage appears to have more than one meaning, the clearest interpretation should be chosen.

Try Key #2

Read Philippians 2:1-8. Based on His concern expressed in verses 1-4, which of the following meanings do you think Paul intended in verses 5-8? _____

A. Christ went all the way to the cross in the substitutional sacrifice of Himself in atonement for mankind's sin.

B. Christ humbled Himself before others and consistently considered human needs above His own rights.

C. Christ was God incarnate in human flesh, and although He was 100 percent God, He also was 100 percent man.

Check your answers with the Answer List in the back of the book.

5.
Historical Setting

 Interpret a Passage in the Light of its Historical Setting.

God has given His special revelation in and through historical situations. The role the historical setting played in shaping the message of a passage must be determined in the study of that passage. You must examine the historical, physical (or geographical), and cultural (social, religious, and material) setting in which the original communication was given, if you are to understand what it meant to the recipients. Most of Scripture is understood best when it is considered in the light of the historical situation of the persons to whom, about whom, and by whom the passage was written.

Understanding the historical background of a passage helps in understanding and interpreting the passage. You may misunderstand a passage if you interpret it according to your present-day culture. Because meanings change from one culture to another, and from one age to another, we need to understand biblical expressions in their cultural context. Once you determine what a passage meant to the people in its historical setting, you can seek to understand what meaning is relevant for you today.

The historical background oftentimes can be found in Scripture itself. For example, the historical narrative of Paul's missionary ministry in Philippi, located in Acts 16:11-40, presents background information for a study of his letter to the Philippians. Likewise, the historical books of the Old Testament provide the historical background of the prophets.

Marginal references in a Study Bible are helpful in locating the historical background of a particular passage. Sometimes extrabiblical historical sources are helpful. Bible study tools that provide such information are the Bible dictionary, encyclopedia, handbook, atlas, and history book.

Try Key #3

In view of the fact that Paul was a prisoner at Rome when he wrote Philippians, what special significance does each of the following verses convey concerning the adequacy of Christ? Read the passages and write your thoughts by each reference here:

• Philippians 1:12-13—

• Philippians 2:25-30—

• Philippians 3:10-14—

• Philippians 4:10-13—

Check your answers with the Answer List in the back of the book.

6.
Purpose and Plan

 Interpret According to the
Author's Purpose and Plan.

Every book of the Bible has a unique *purpose*, even though it shares the broad purpose of all the Bible books—the revelation of God and His redemptive program. To ascertain the purpose of the Bible book under study is essential to the interpreter. The purpose of the author is the objective he had in mind when writing.

Sometimes the purpose is stated within the book itself, as in John 20:31 and Revelation 1:1-3. Most of the time, however, one must read through the entire book and discover the flow of thought in order to discern what the purpose is. A comparison of Bible study tools (study Bible, Bible handbook, Bible introduction book, and Bible commentary) will aid you in understanding the purpose.

Almost always the author of a Bible book has a *plan* for developing his theme. There is a logical connection from one section of the book to another. The plan may be historical or poetical, chronological or topical, systematic or random. The plan of the author is the way the material is organized to carry out the author's purpose. To interpret an individual passage properly, you must consider it in accordance with the author's broader plan. Each thought must be interpreted in connection with adjoining thoughts.

Making an outline of a book is most helpful in establishing the plan and purpose of the book in one's thinking. Changes in thought, transitions, and relationships of ideas must be studied in composing an outline; and each major heading must be viewed in its relationship to the major theme of the book.

When the purpose and plan of the book is determined, you will be prepared for considering each passage in the light of its broader context.

Try Key #4

Read the following verses in Philippians, and from these deduce what you think is the major *theme* of the book: Philippians 1:7,12,18; 2:1-2,29-30; 3:1,10; 4:1,4,10-14.
Theme: _____
Compose a brief *outline* of Philippians by deciding on a major heading for each division of the book as indicated below (A check of the particular verses indicated in the parentheses will help you in deciding on the headings):

I. Chap. 1:1-11, _____
(See especially 1:3,9)

II. Chap. 1:12-26, _____
(See especially 1:12,13,23-25)

III. Chaps. 1:27-2:18, _____
(See especially 1:27; 2:5,15)

IV. Chap. 2:19-30, _____
(See especially 2:19,20,25,28)

V. Chap. 3:1-4:7, _____
(See especially 3:2,17,18)

VI. Chap. 4:2-23, _____
(See especially 4:2,4,9,14-16)

Check your answers with the Answer List in the back
of the book.

7.
Word Meaning

 Interpret the Correct Meaning
of Individual Words.

A word is the smallest unit of thought and communication. Human language is comprised of words. Words are basic building blocks of a passage of Scripture. The words of Scriptures must be understood if the Word of God is to be understood.

The Bible student remembers that the Old Testament is translated from Hebrew and the New Testament from Greek (and some Aramaic). He or she remembers, furthermore, that the English language itself has undergone changes since the *King James Version* of 1611.

We face certain problems with words. Rarely does a word in one language mean precisely the same thing in another language. In studying the Scripture, therefore, it is necessary to make a direct study of every crucial word to make sure that it is translated properly in English. Because some words have profound meaning, the student must determine the range of meaning and the proper meaning with each use. Several words in the original language may be translated into the same English word, and the student must learn the shade of meaning in each case.

What thoughts come to your mind as you read the following four words: *Perfect-Lights-Beware-Riches*? Now notice how your thoughts change as you read each of these as they appear in four phrases in Philippians: "He who began a good work in you will *perfect* it until the day of Christ Jesus" (1:6); "A crooked and perverse generation, among whom you appear as *lights* in the world" (2:15); "*Beware* of the evil workers" (3:2); "And my God shall supply all your needs according to His *riches* in glory in Christ Jesus" (4:19).

This little exercise should point up three facts about words:

(1) A word standing alone rarely is clear: it needs additional words to formulate a clear idea. (2) A word becomes clear as we understand how an author is using it. You must carefully search to determine what meaning the author had in mind when he used the word. (3) A word must be considered in its context. A careful study of the passage in which a word occurs usually will enable you to find some key to the meaning of the word.

Walter Henrichsen suggests four things that must be determined in the study of a specific word: (1) its use by the author, (2) its relation to its immediate context, (3) its current use at the time of writing, and (4) its root meaning.[6]

Try Key #5

Can you interpret the correct meaning of these three words in Philippians?

1. The word *always* does not mean the same thing in Philippians 1:4 as it means in Matthew 28:20. Read each verse and state what you think *always* means in each case.

 a. Matthew 28:20 _____

 b. Philippians 1:4 (compare with 1:3) _____

2. In Philippians 1:20-24, Paul speaks of *death*. Actually, his thoughts help us to formulate a definition of *death*. Write a definition of *death* based on Paul's concepts in this passage.

_____

_____

Check your answer with two additional verses: 2 Corinthians 5:8 and James 2:26.

3. Does the word *perfect* in Philippians 3:15 mean "absolute lack of any sin or flaw?" Yes _____ No _____ Check the context before this verse (vv. 12-14) and write your definition of *perfect* as Paul used it here: _____

_____

Check your answers with the Answer List in the back of the book.

8.
Grammar

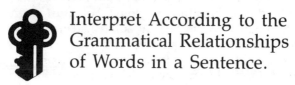 Interpret According to the Grammatical Relationships of Words in a Sentence.

Different words are linked together in a sentence to form a thought structure. The thought structure is governed by grammatical laws. Grammar is defined by Webster as "the system of word structures and word arrangements of a given language at a given time." The biblical languages usually are more precise than English. The Bible student must diligently endeavor to discover the grammatical relationships of words in the text that he or she studies.

Two basic matters to note in grammatical interpretation are the position of each word in the sentence and the relationship of each word to others in the sentence. A knowledge of parts of speech is necessary for grammatical inter-preparation. When studying the sentences in a passage, identify the *subject*. Study each *verb*, considering its tense. Determine what each *adjective* and *adverb* describes and how it describes it. Note how *prepositions, genitives,* and *conjunctions* relate words to each other. Find the *antecedent* (word to which it refers) of each pronoun.

J. Robertson McQuilkin has suggested some basic questions to ask in the grammatical analysis of a passage:

1. *What or who is the main subject of the thought?* The subject will be a noun, or a pronoun or a phrase standing in place of the noun.

2. *What action does the subject do?* The verb indicates the action, state, or condition, and is called the predicate.

3. *What or who is the object of the action?* This can be either a direct object or an indirect object.

4. *How have the parts of the thought been modified by a word or a phrase?* Modifiers include adjectives and adverbs.

5. *What are the relationships among the various parts of the thought?* Prepositions and conjunctions are words indicating relationship.

6. *How does the key idea or thought relate to those before and after it?*[7]

One who does not have a knowledge of the original languages will be dependent upon the translators and commentators in making a grammatical analysis of a scriptural passage. When studying a passage, consult and compare different translations and several good critical commentaries (that is, commentaries dealing more with the authenticity and language of the original text).

Try Key #6

1. *Check this word position.* Philippians 4:6 in English reads, "Be anxious for nothing." In the Greek it reads, "Nothing be anxious about." What emphasis can you draw from the Greek reading? _____

_____

2. *Check This Word Relationship.* Read Philippians 1:6 and state here the way you interpret and apply the verse: _____

_____

_____

You probably did not know that the singular *you* and the plural *you* are indicated by different endings in the Greek (This is not the case in English). The *you* in verse 6 is plural. To whom, then, does the plural *you* refer? (See verse 1)

_____

Now check the most appropriate of the following two interpretations: _____ (a) God promises me that He will complete the good work He has begun in me. _____ (b) God promises His church that His work in her will continue, and she will prevail.

Check your answers with the Answer List in the back of the book.

9.
Context

Interpret a Passage in the Light of Its Context.

Contextual interpretation asks the question: How does the passage relate to the material surrounding it? *Context* means the unit of thought in which a word or passage appears. Context is the entire body of writing in which a particular idea is located. By observing what precedes and follows a passage, one is able to interpret more accurately the idea that the writer sought to convey to the original readers.

The "immediate context" should include the paragraph in which a verse appears, and it may include two or three preceding paragraphs and two or three following paragraphs. The interpreter must read carefully around the passage to determine where the thought begins and where it ends. These two points, then, mark the immediate context.

Any word must be interpreted in the light of its context. A word may have different meanings in different passages. Knowledge of how a word is used in other places in the Bible may be of help in determining its meaning in a particular passage. However, the context of the word provides, in almost every case, the most help in determining the word's meaning.

A verse also must be considered in its context in order to get the progress of thought and the intent of the verse. Connections between words and thoughts must be noted as the context is studied. To insist, "Don't take the verse out of its context" is to respect the necessity of giving the appropriate meaning and application to the verse in the light of its context. One way to determine how well you understand a verse in its context is to write your own paraphrase of the entire passage. See how well you can express the thought in your own words while you tie together all the ideas of the passage. The meaning of a passage must be determined by its flow of thought.

The "wider context" of a passage is the larger body of material surrounding it outside its immediate unit of thought. As a word and verse must be considered in the light of the immediate context of a paragraph, a paragraph has to be considered in the light of the wider context of the chapter and the entire Bible book. The Bible book must be considered in the light of the teaching of the entire Bible. The context of a word is the sentence in which it appears. The context of the sentence is its paragraph, whose context is its chapter, whose context is its book, whose context is the whole Bible.

The consideration of context is important in all of Bible study. One may make an erroneous interpretation and faulty application of a Bible verse if one neglects to interpret it in the light of its context. To faithfully adhere to context is expressive of the interpreter's respect for the authority of Scripture. Perhaps the context is the most important means we have of determining the meaning of a word or passage.

Mickelsen listed the following principles for interpreting from context:

1. Observe carefully the immediate context—that which precedes and follows the passage.

2. Observe carefully any parallels in the same book to the materials in the passage being interpreted. Be aware of the purposes and development of thought in the book.

3. Observe carefully any parallel in another book by the same author or in other books by different authors. Take into account the purpose and development of thought in these books.

4. Where the immediate context is of little or no value, try to find genuine parallels which come from the same period or time.

5. Bear in mind that the smaller the quantity of material to be interpreted, the greater the danger of ignoring context. No axiom is better known and more frequently disobeyed than the oft quoted: "A text without a context is only a pretext." Somehow, to discern this kind of error in someone else is easy but to recognize this same fault in ourselves is most difficult.[8]

There are only a few areas of the Bible in which the context may not be a great deal of help in interpretation. Job, Proverbs, and Ecclesiastes in the Wisdom Literature oftentimes present brief sayings of various kinds that express a single thought and do not relate to the context. In such cases, parallels may be found elsewhere that can be studied to see what help they provide in interpretation.

Try Key #7

Now for an example from Philippians that indicates how the context helps to determine the meaning of a biblical word. Paul used the word *flesh* in several ways in his epistles. Oftentimes it is used in reference to the whole human personality that is bent toward earthly pursuits rather than the will of God. Romans 8:1-13 uses *flesh* in this way. Paul contrasted "flesh" with "spirit" and declared that "if you are living according to the flesh, you must die" (v. 13); but in Philippians 1:20-24, Paul used "flesh" with a different meaning. Read all of this passage and state what is meant by "flesh" here according to the context:_____

Check your answers with the Answer List in the back of the book.

10.
Related Scripture

 Interpret Scripture by Scripture.

An important means of assuring a correct interpretation of a passage is to consult related passages within the Scriptures, that is, passages that are parallel in thought or event, or in which there are points of similarity or complementary contrast. The Bible itself is the best commentary on the Bible.

The benefits of comparing Scripture with Scripture are stated by McQuilkin: "To compare the passage under study with other passages of Scripture will often clarify meaning, correct an initial understanding, or bring the teaching to completion as part of the biblical whole."[9]

The Bible forms a unit. It does not contradict itself, it complements itself. The New Testament is a commentary on the Old Testament. The two testaments are two parts of the same book, not two separate books. The New Testament Epistles amplify the seed doctrines of the Gospels and Acts. Parallel passages are found in two or more of the Gospels; Samuel and Kings are parallel to Chronicles; portions of Ephesians and Colossians compare; and portions of Romans and Galatians are similar. All sixty-six books of the Bible form essential parts of God's progressive revelation. Though His disclosure of Himself to human beings is progressive, God's character is the same in every age, and His requirements and plans for human lives are the same. It is wise, therefore, to consult verses in different parts of the Bible that discuss the same thing. Almost any doctrinal passage in Scripture has a parallel somewhere else in Scripture.

Not only should a passage be compared with other passages that have similar teaching, it also should be compared with other passages that have contrasting teaching, as McQuilkin suggested:

> Many times a passage cannot be fully understood until the teaching has been compared with contrasting teaching in other passages. Since commitment to the trustworthiness of Scripture means that there can be no ultimate conflict, an attempt must be able to resolve apparent conflicts[10]

For example,

> Christ said, "Do not judge lest you be judged" (Matt. 7:1). Paul emphasized the same truth: "Who are you to judge the servant of another?" (Rom. 14:4). Many have taken that as an absolute norm for Christian conduct, insisting that no Christian may ever judge another human being. However, there are contrasting passages, one of which is also in the Sermon on the Mount: "Beware of the false prophets. . . . you will know them by their fruits" (Matt. 7:15-16). In fact, Christ said directly, "Judge with righteous judgment" (John 7:24), and John reinforces that: "Test the spirits to see whether they are from God. . . . By this we know the spirit of truth and the spirit of error" (1 John 4:1,6). To understand all God would teach us concerning judging and refraining from judging others, a systematic study must be made of all biblical teaching on the subject. However, at this point, it is important to note that neither of those teachings can be rightly understood without reference to contrasting passages.[11]

You cannot fully understand the message of the Bible on a particular subject until you have considered all that the Bible says on the subject. Before you draw firm conclusions regarding a teaching that is merely implied in a Scripture passage, compare it with related passages. If the related passages support the implied teaching, then it may be considered biblical.

Adhering to the basic principle of interpreting Scripture by Scripture can save you from error and heresy, as Norton Sterrett stated:

Heresies and false doctrines seem to have biblical authority because those who teach them use only certain passages and ignore others. We can be kept from believing wrong doctrine by checking our understanding of a verse by the message of the whole Bible. We should maintain a humble attitude and not be quick to form final or dogmatic conclusions about the meaning of one verse until we have considered it in the light of the whole Word of God.[12]

Use the cross-references in a study Bible to locate passages related to the passage under study. A cross-reference book such as *Treasury of Scripture Knowledge* would list even more cross-references. If the topic you are studying is doctrinal, a theology book on the subject will offer additional help in locating both similar and contrasting passages.

A grasp of the message of the Bible as a whole and an understanding of the key message and subthemes of each Bible book will enable you to become proficient in comparing Scripture with Scripture. You should, therefore, dedicate yourself to the faithful study of God's Word. Make a good overall survey of the Bible first. Then get into book studies. Maintain a regular study of the Word throughout your life. If you are faithful in a systematic study of the Scriptures, you will find that your knowledge of the Word is growing continually; and you will be alert to discover related Scriptures.

Try Key #8

In Philippians 3:3, Paul claimed that he and his readers "are the true circumcision." Trace the use of the term *circumcision* through several other passages of Scripture to obtain a fuller meaning of the term.

A. What nation had circumcision as a seal of their covenant relationship with God (Acts 7:5-8); Rom. 4:9-12; Eph. 2:11)?

_____

B. Did this term also apply to a group of Jews who professed faith in Jesus Christ (Acts 10:45; Gal. 2:11-12)?
☐ Yes ☐ No _____

C. Did this group remain true to the gospel of grace (Titus 1:10-11; Acts 11:2-3)? _____

D. What false teaching did the "circumcision" group propagate (Acts 15:1; Gal. 2:3-4; 6:12-15)? _____

E. What did Paul mean here in Philippians 3:3 when he said that the true worshipers of Jesus Christ are the "circumcision" (Col. 2:11; Rom. 2:29)? _____

Check your answers with the Answer List in the back of the book.

Part III
Compartment Keys: Special Hermeneutics

The eight principles of Bible interpretation covered in the previous "keys" are classified as "general hermeneutics." They are laws that apply generally in the study of any passage of Scripture. The seven principles that we now will cover relate to special types of material contained in the Scriptures, and fit the classification of "special hermeneutics."

Special forms and themes that occur in the Bible are figures of speech, symbols and types, parables and allegory, Hebrew poetry, and prophecy. Special principles are needed for interpreting these special forms and themes. This is where "special hermeneutics" come in. Mickelsen specifies the function of special hermeneutics as follows: "Special hermeneutics deals with definitions and principles which make it easier to interpret special literary forms or to convey the meaning found in specific topical areas treated in the biblical material."[13]

Special hermeneutics, therefore, deals with the principles that help us to understand special types of language.

11.
Figures of Speech

 Recognize Figures of Speech and Interpret Them According to the Author's Intention

To declare that "I must cram this book into my head" does not mean that I must literally cut open my cranium and literally stuff the book into my head. It means that I sense the necessity of gaining an understanding of the concepts taught in the book. The language employed to communicate the idea is called "figurative language." We all use figurative language frequently.

Figurative Language

"Figurative language" refers to words and concepts that are used with meaning other than their ordinary, natural sense. All languages employ figurative means of expressing ideas. The Bible is replete with figurative language. Jesus used much figurative language to describe His relationship to His people and His spiritual provisions for them. Figurative language is the flower of rhetoric. It gives beauty and fragrance to speech. For instance, the use of a metaphor in saying that "the Lord is my shepherd" is a more picturesque way for David, the tender of sheep, to express God's loving care for him than saying, "The Lord directs my life." Figurative language is used to give pictorial representation to intended meanings. The images of figurative language are borrowed from daily life to give impressive and accurate descriptions of spiritual truth.

Figurative language does not violate the principles of literal interpretation because even figures of speech build on their literal antecedents. Most of the Bible uses literal language. Various kinds of figurative language, however, appear throughout the Bible. The literal approach to interpretation recognizes figurative language and interprets it according to the literal idea intended by the author.

The figurative language of the Bible includes figures of speech (the most common), the Hebrew idiom, symbol, type, parable, and allegory. It is necessary that you be able to identify the type of literature or language in a passage and to interpret it according to the guidelines for understanding that type of language. This lesson will deal with figures of speech. In figurative language, the thing to which the author refers, as a general rule, is identified by only one simple characteristic of the figure used. This is especially true of figures of speech.

Figures of Speech

An English handbook defines *figures of speech* as "expressions of comparison, analogy, personification that are used to intensify statements, to make them more expressive and vivid."[14]

Some figurative statements found in the first chapter of Philippians are (author's emphasis):
- v:6 - "He who began a good *work* in you"
- v:7 - "I have you in my *heart*"
- v:11 - "Having been filled with the *fruit* of righteousness"
- v:20 - "Be exalted in my *body*"
- v:21 - "For to me, *to live is Christ*"
- v:23 - "I am *hard-pressed* from both *directions*"
- v:27 - "That you are *standing* firm in one spirit"

Guidelines for Interpreting Figures of Speech
- First, a literal interpretation would be absurd.
- Second, you must learn the qualities that the author knew the figure to have.

• Third, you must determine the quality the author must have had in mind.

• Fourth, you must study the context to confirm the appropriateness of your interpretation.

For example, when John called Christ "the lamb of God," you will know that a literal interpretation would be absurd. Christ was not a four-legged animal. You will sort the possibilities: John may have had in mind the quality of humility or of proneness to stray or of the substitute offering for sin. You decide that the latter quality is the one John had in mind. The context of John's life and ministry will confirm that he was referring to Christ as the Messiah who would fulfill the role of which the sacrificial lamb was a type. You settle, therefore, on the last interpretation as the most fitting.

Two Keys to Identify and Interpret Figurative Language

Irving Jensen suggested that common sense and context are two key helpers in identifying and interpreting figurative language:

Since such important spiritual truths are conveyed by figurative language, it is essential that the Bible student become proficient in the interpretation of such language. His task is twofold: (1) to ascertain what is figurative in a passage, and (2) to determine the truth intended by the original author through that figure— no more and no less. In most passages, the student should have no serious difficulty with either task. (The Book of Revelation is a notable exception.)

For the first task, he should follow the sound interpretative principle that words should be interpreted literally unless this leads to contradiction or absurdity. Common-sense judgment is necessary here.

For the second task, that of determining what spiritual truth is being taught by the figure of speech, the student needs to identify the picture for which the *context* is calling. For example, the word "shepherd" could in a certain context emphasize the *lowly* aspect of such a man's occupation. However, for the phrase, "The Lord is my shepherd," the context of the twenty-third Psalm indicates that the *guidance, protection* and *provision* aspects of shepherding are being taught.

Common sense and context, then, are the two key helpmates in identifying the Biblical author's intentions in his use of literal and figurative language.[15]

Let's take from Philippians another example of a figure of speech. When Paul warned the Philippians, "Beware of the dogs" (Phil. 3:2), he used a figure of speech. The "dogs" were Judaizers who insisted on imposing on Gentile Christians all the ordinances of the Old Testament. "Dogs" was an impressive term to Paul's readers, and its description of the evil and harmful Judaizers was accurate. The Judaizers were to Christians what real dogs were to people in general in Paul's day. Dogs were considered very unclean by Jews because they were the common scavengers in the Oriental cities. The Judaizers who opposed the message of salvation by grace actually were destructive of God's work in the lives of potential believers and immature believers. Paul warned against them. The context reveals what Paul meant by his use of the term "dogs" when speaking of the Judaizers. In the same verse, he called them "evil workers"—their work was harmful and evil, like that of scavenger dogs. He also called them "the concision" (KJV, mutilation; translated "false circumcision" in the NASB)—their insistence on the ordinance of circumcision as essential to salvation was a multilation of the doctrine of grace, like the dogs' mutilation of flesh.

Following are definitions[16] and biblical examples of ten figures of speech. Of the many figures found in the Bible, these are the ones most often used and most necessary to understand.

Figures of Comparison

1. *Simile*—one thing is likened to another, dissimilar thing by the use of *like* or *as*: "All of us like sheep have gone astray" (Isa. 53:6); "behold, I send you out as lambs in the midst of wolves" (Luke 10:3).

2. *Metaphor*—implied comparison in which a word or phrase ordinarily and primarily used of one thing is applied to another: "I have other sheep, which are not of this fold; I must bring them also, and they shall hear My voice; and they shall become one flock with one shepherd" (John 10:16).

Figures of Relation

3. *Metonymy*—use of the name of one thing for that of another associated with or suggested by it: "They have Moses and the Prophets; let them hear them" (Luke 16:29). "Moses and the prophets" stand for the writings of Moses and the writings of the prophets in the Old Testament.

4. *Synecdoche*—a part is used for a whole, an individual for a class, a singular for a plural, or the reverse of one of these: "Israel has sinned, and they have also transgressed My covenant which I commanded them. And they have even taken some of the things under the ban and have both stolen and deceived" (Josh. 7:11). The sin to which God referred is that of Achan, who stole forbidden spoils and hid them in his tent. All Israel was affected by Achan's sin. God said "Israel has sinned," though the sin was that of one person. The figure used is a whole for a part, or a class for an individual.

Figures of Humanization

5. *Anthropomorphism*—the attributing of human shape or characteristics to God. Though an anthropomorphism may be the attributing of an inanimate object, an animal, or a natural phenomena to God, in the Scriptures the anthropomorphism is almost always the attributing of *human* features to God: "Behold, the Lord's hand is not so short/That it cannot save; /Neither is His ear so dull/That it cannot hear" (Isa. 59:1). An *anthropopathism* is used to ascribe to God human emotions and responses: "Who knows, God may turn and relent, and withdraw His burning anger so that we shall not perish?" (Jonah 3:9).

6. *Personification*—a thing, quality, or idea is represented as a person: "Then when lust has conceived, it gives birth to sin;

and when sin is accomplished, it brings forth death" (Jas. 1:15).

7. *Apostrophe*—words addressed to a person or thing, whether absent or present, generally in an exclamatory tone and as a digression in a speech or literary writing: "Again He said to me, 'Prophesy over these bones, and say to them, 'O dry bones, hear the word of the Lord'" (Ezek. 37:4).

In an apostrophe, the speaker or writer emotionally imagines that he or she is turning from the audience to directly address another person, thing, or abstract idea. The speaker is thinking out loud, as it were, and the object of the speaker's thoughts most likely is not physically present. David's lament was addressed to his son, not only absent but dead: "O my son Absalom, my son, my son Absalom! would God I had died for thee, O Absalom, my son, my son!" (2 Sam. 18:33 KJV). The Old Testament prophets used the apostrophe often, as in Isaiah 54:1: "Shout for joy, O barren one." The context shows that Isaiah is speaking to a nation, not to a woman.

The apostrophe often appears somewhat parenthetical and is expressed generally as an exclamation. In the midst of his glorious teaching on the resurrection, Paul exclaimed to Death, "O death, where is thy sting? O grave, where is thy victory?" (I Cor. 15:55 KJV).

Probably you have noticed from some of the verses quoted above that an apostrophe is clearly related to personification. Sometimes a figure is both an apostrophe and a personification, as in Psalm 114:5-6: "What ailed thee, O thou sea, that thou fleddest? thou Jordan, that thou wast driven back? Ye mountains, that ye skipped like rams; and ye little hills, like lambs?" (KJV). Again, the psalmist exclaimed to the mountain as though it could hear and think: "Why do you look with envy, O/mountains with many peaks" (Ps. 68:16). This is both personification and apostrophe.

Figures of Intensification

8. *Hyperbole*—exaggeration for effect, not meant to be taken literally: "There are also many other things which Jesus did,

which if they were written in detail, I suppose that even the world itself would not contain the books which were written" (John 21:25).

9. *Irony*—humorous or subtly sarcastic expression in which the intended meaning of the words used is the direct opposite of their usual sense: "You are already filled, you have already become rich, you have become kings without us; and I would indeed that you had become kings so that we might reign with you" (1 Cor. 4:8). In their independence and indifference to the feelings of their fellow Christians, the Corinthians acted as though they had arrived; but Paul here rebuked their attitude as vain imagination.

10. *Rhetorical question*—a question to which no answer is expected, or to which only one obvious answer may be made: "Behold, I am the Lord, the God of all flesh; is anything too difficult for Me?" (Jer. 32:27). The rhetorical question is a means of focusing the thought upon a central idea to intensify that idea.

Try Key #9

Match each of the following terms with its appropriate definition. Then check your answers with the definitions above.

_____ 1. Anthropomorphism   A. exaggeration for effect, not meant to be taken literally

_____ 2. Hyperbole   B. the attributing of human shape or characteristics to God

_____ 3. Irony   C. use of the name of one thing for that of another associated with or suggested by it.

_____4. Metonymy   D. a question to which one
                                 answer is expected and one
                                 answer is obvious
_____5. Rhetorical question   E. humorous or subtly sar-
                                 castic expression in which
                                 the intended meaning of the
                                 words used is the direct op-
                                 posite of their usual sense

Look up each of the following Scripture verses and identify
the name of the figure of speech that is found in the verse
(You may check the definitions given previously as you determine your answer):

6. Psalm 1:3 _____   9. Jeremiah 25:29b _____
7. Psalm 98:8 _____   10. John 1:36 _____
8. Jeremiah 22:29 _____

Check your answers with the Answer List in the back
of the book.

12.
Symbol

 Find the Single Representative
Meaning of a Symbol.

The words *symbol, type,* and *allegory* are closely related. Each is a figure of speech extended.

Webster defines *symbol* as "something that stands for or represents another thing; esp., an object used to represent something abstract."[17] A symbol is a common item from everyday life that is used in speech to convey a special meaning about some spiritual truth. A symbol is used to represent another thing because of some resemblance that it bears to that thing. Often, it is a material or physical object that is used to represent an immaterial truth. A symbol has a representative meaning as well as its ordinary one. For example, a dove may represent the Holy Spirit while it also is a beautiful white bird. The cross may represent salvation while it also is a wooden instrument of execution.

A number of kinds of things are used as symbols in Scripture such as objects, creatures, actions, ordinances, materials, names, numbers, and colors. The cross is the most common symbol in the New Testament, a pictorial representation of the historical death of Christ as the source of salvation for all humanity. The bread and wine of the Lord's Supper are symbols of the atoning death and new covenant provided by Christ (1 Cor. 11:24-25).

The Passover forever afterwards was symbolic of God's powerful deliverance of His people. Israel's passing through the Red Sea (Ex. 14:22) symbolized her break with Egypt and her commitment to obey God (1 Cor. 10:4). The rock from which Israel drank (Num. 20:11) was symbolic of Christ the Provider (1 Cor. 10:2).

Sometimes symbolic actions were used in the Old Testament to illustrate doctrinal or prophetical truths. In such cases, men of God not only proclaimed their message but performed actions that demonstrated future workings of God. For example, Jeremiah buried a new waistband in the earth and later dug it up, spoiled, to represent how Israel was going to be rejected by God and despoiled (Jer. 13:4-5).

Sometimes symbols were objects seen in visions, as in the case of Zechariah's vision of the golden candlestick with a bowl on the top from which seven pipes brought oil for seven lamps (Zech. 4:1-14). The candlestick symbolized Israel as God's lights in the world, and the oil represented the Holy Spirit as the source of energy.

Numbers oftentimes are symbolic in Scripture. For example, the number *seven* often carries a force of completion, perfection, and totality. The number *three* often relates to the Trinity, *four* to physical creation, and *forty* to a period of testing; but because the Bible nowhere actually says that these numbers are symbolic, one must be careful not to press too strongly when interpreting the significance of numbers in the Scriptures. We must not read extra meaning into a verse when no indication exists that it is there.

In interpreting a Bible symbol, carefully note how the Bible itself interprets it. Note the natural qualities of the symbol, and determine which one fits the meaning of the passage you are studying. Look for an explanation of the meaning in the context of the passage under study. Use a concordance to look up the word in as many verses as you can to determine how the Bible interprets the particular symbol.

Sometimes the writer explains the symbol that he has used. Where the writer does not explain his meaning, it becomes the responsibility of the interpreter to find out what the symbol originally was meant to teach.

Be careful not to make symbols out of things spoken of in Scripture that are not meant to be symbolic. Be aware, also, that the same object may symbolize one thing in one Scripture but something different in another Scripture.

Mickelsen has provided the following principles for interpreting symbols:

1. Note the qualities of the literal object denoted by the symbol.

2. Try to discover from the context the purpose for using a symbol.

3. Use any explanation given in the context to connect the symbol and the truth it teaches. If the symbol is not explained, then use every clue found in the immediate context or in any part of the book where the figure occurs. Try to state why the symbol was effective for the first hearers or readers.

4. If a symbol which was clear to the initial readers is not clear to modern readers, state explicitly what the barrier is for the modern reader. Where there is uncertainty of meaning, the interpreter should proceed from those factors of which he is the most sure. Only the man who is wise in his own judgment (cf. Rom. 12:16) has all the answers on symbols. We should always strive to improve our understanding of symbols where uncertainty prevails and where our decision as to meaning is tentative.

5. Observe the frequency and distribution of a symbol (how often and where found), but allow each context to control the meaning. Do not force symbols into preconceived schemes of uniformity.

6. Think or meditate upon your results. The reason Paul could glory or boast in the cross of Christ (Gal. 6:14) is that he knew what this symbol stood for. Meditation always precedes such a response.[18]

The key, therefore, to finding the single representative meaning of a symbol is to determine how the Bible context itself interprets the symbol.

Try Key #10

Look up the following six Scripture passages. For each, identify in the blank the symbol that is used.

1. Genesis 3:24: symbol of the rupture of fellowship between God and humanity:_____

2. Exodus 3:2: symbol of the presence of God: _____

3. Deuteronomy 12:23-25: symbol of life: _____

4. Jeremiah 24:1-10: symbol of the group that went to Babylon and the group that stayed in Judah: good and bad

_____

5. Ezekiel 1:15-21: symbol of the function of the cherubim:

_____

6. Revelation 6:1: symbol of judgments: opening of seven

_____

Check your answers with the Answer List in the back of the book.

13.
Type

 Interpret a Type According to Its New Testament Explanation.

A *type* is a person, thing, or event that represents another that will appear after it. A type is an Old Testament prefiguring of something about redemption in the New Testament, as the Old Testament sacrifices are foreshadows of the sacrificial, redemptive work of Christ in His crucifixion. Both the type and the antitype (that which is foreshadowed by the type) are always actual historical persons, things, or events. The type embodies characteristics (and there may be more than one in a type) that later appear in the antitype.

An example of a type and the characteristics common with its antitype is presented by Mickelsen:

> For example, the experience of the children of Israel being bitten by serpents in the desert is handled typologically in the New Testament. The Old Testament account in Numbers 21:6-9 tells that fiery serpents were sent among the people. The serpents bit the people and caused many of them to die. Moses made a bronze serpent and set it on a pole. Everyone bitten by a serpent who looked at the model recovered.

> In John 3:14, this Old Testament event is said to be a "type" of the New Testament event of Christ's death upon a cross: "And as Moses lifted up the serpent in the wilderness, so must the Son of man be lifted up, that whoever believes in him may have eternal life."

> Points of correspondence are: (1) the lifting up of the serpent and of Christ, and (2) life for those who respond to the object lifted up. In both points the typology makes a higher applica-

tion of meaning than the original. Both the serpent and Christ were literally lifted up. Both events occurred in history. But the meaning of the "lifting up" of Christ in crucifixion is infinitely greater. The same is true of the response. Those who looked at the bronze serpent "lived" in the sense that they did not then die of snakebite. Those who commit themselves to Christ have "eternal life," a new quality of life both in the now and in the life to come.[19]

A type may be viewed as one sort of prophetic symbol. Whereas a symbol may represent something past, present, or future, a type always points to something future. Usually, only one point of similarity is intended between a symbol and the thing symbolized. The point of similarity may change from the time it is used by the author to another time. A type points to one particular antitype and may represent a number of points of similarity in its antitype.

Sterrett summarized the difference between symbols and types as follows:

1. A type is actual (historical) while a symbol may not be.

2. A type is in the Old Testament with its fulfillment in the New. A symbol has no time reference.

3. A type is particular (one thing or event). A symbol may be general.

4. A type may have some details, though not usually. A symbol has one point.

5. A type may contain one or more symbols.[20]

Spiritualizing is highly possible in the area of typology. One must be careful to allow the Scripture to be the authority in the designation of types. In a book on the life of Joseph, the son of Jacob, I have pointed out fourteen similarities between Joseph and Jesus Christ. Yet I was careful not to insist that Joseph is a "type" of Christ, because the Scripture nowhere indicates Joseph to be a type. One should not vest an illustration or application with biblical authority by calling it a type when the Scripture does not give it that designation. This is a safe guideline, as McQuilkin stated:

> If the Bible does not identify something as being typical, it may still be legitimate to draw parallels and use the object, the event, or the person as an illustration, but it is questionable to designate it as a type.[21]

Some of the persons of the Old Testament who are referred to in the New Testament as types of Christ are Melchizedek (Gen. 14:17-20; Ps. 110:4; Heb. 7:1-11), David (Ps. 69:9; John 2:16-17; Rom. 15:3), Solomon (2 Sam. 7:12-14; Heb. 1:5), Isaiah (Isa. 8:16; Heb. 2:13), and Jonah (Jonah 1:17; Matt. 12:39-41; 16:4).

Events of the Old Testament such as the Sabbath rest, Rachel's grief, Israel's call out of Egypt, and the Passover are treated as types in the New Testament. Things such as the temple and instruction in parables also are treated typically. The tabernacle and its pieces of furniture are viewed as typical of the spiritual provisions of Christ (Heb. 9-10).

To interpret a type, you first must determine whether it is indicated by Scripture to be a type. Next, look for an explanation within the Scripture contexts. Then, determine which qualities of the type illustrate characteristics of the antitype.

Try Key #11

Take a look at Melchizedek as a type of Christ:

1. Psalm 110:4 compares Melchizedek and the one addressed as Lord. This comparison is applied to Christ several times in Hebrews 5:6,10; 6:20; 7:11,17. What phrase is repeated in all these verses? _____

2. What is the main point about Christ that is taught by the comparison? (See Heb. 7:3,21,23-25) _____

3. The following facts about Melchizedek may be drawn from a study of Genesis 14:17-20:

    a. His beginning and end are not recorded

    b. Priest of God Most High prior to the Aaronic priesthood

    c. King of Salem (earlier name of Jerusalem); Salem means
       "peace"
    d. His name means "king of righteousness"
    e. Brought forth bread and wine
    f. Blessed Abraham on behalf of the Most High God
    g. Ascribed blessing to God for the victory granted to
       Abraham
    h. Abraham gave to him the tenth part of the spoil
    i. Met Abraham following Abraham's battle

Circle the letter of each fact above that is cited in Hebrews 7:1-10 where Melchizedek is presented as a type of Jesus Christ.

Check your answers with the Answer List in the back of the book.

14.
Parable and Allegory

 Find the Central Teaching of a Parable and Distinguish it from an Allegory.

Jesus often used parables in His teaching. Matthew 13:34 says, "All these things Jesus spoke to the multitudes in parables, and He did not speak to them without a parable." Do you recognize the figure of speech Matthew uses? It is a hyperbole, an exaggeration for effect. He obviously meant that parables were Christ's chief means of communication.

The Parable

A *parable* is an earthly story that illustrates a heavenly truth. Robert C. McQuilkin offered this definition: "A parable is an outside story with an inside meaning."[22] A fuller definition follows: "A parable is a brief story or narrative drawn from human life or from nature, not relating to some actual event, but true to life and concerning something very familiar to the listeners, given for the purpose of teaching a spiritual truth."[23]

The parable is not an example: it only illustrates the truth. It teaches a spiritual truth alongside its story, but the truth is separate from the story. It teaches a spiritual truth through similarities but does not incorporate its meaning in the parable itself. The meaning has to be discovered by the hearer.

Some parables are found in the Old Testament, but most are found in the first three Gospels. Christ used parables as a means of jolting people to see things in a different way and to lay hold of important principles.

The parables of Christ are understood best as they are viewed in relation to Christ's key teaching, the kingdom of God, as Mickelsen pointed out:

> The parables cannot be studied apart from the total teachings of Christ. Because parables usually focus on one main point of comparison, this chief point must be related to the central idea of Jesus' message.
>
> *The reign of God* was the center of Jesus' message. The Greek word *basileia*, which designates the royal reign or Kingdom of God, appears more than a hundred times in the Gospels. The parables illustrated and unfolded various aspects of the reign of God.[24]

Jesus' parables are unique. While revealing spiritual truths to those whose hearts are open to receive His message, the parables at the same time conceal the truths from those whose hearts are closed to Christ. Christ indicated this two-fold purpose in answering the disciples' question: "Why do You speak to them in parables?" (Matt. 13:10-17). Christ's parables were intended to make spiritual truths more easily understandable to those who were receptive and to obscure truth for those who had a mind-set of rejection.

As you will see in the exercise below, there are three parts in the context of a parable—the *setting*, the *story*, and the *spiritual application*. Usually you will find all three parts presented in the Scriptures. The surrounding context will offer you light for your interpretation of a parable.

Virtually every parable has a historical occasion that forms the setting for the telling of the story. Examine the setting to determine what experience brought on the parable. The reason that prompted the telling of the parable probably will be seen in the attitude and spiritual condition of the original hearers. For example, Jesus told the parable of the good Samaritan to an expert in the Mosaic law who "wishing to justify himself, . . . said to Jesus, 'And who is my neighbor?'" (Luke 10:29).

Look for the spiritual application made by the storyteller and the effect the story had upon the hearers. Sometimes at the end of a parable there is a brief statement of its teaching. For example, following His parable of the good Samaritan, Jesus asked, "Which of these three do you think proved to be a neighbor to the man who fell into the robbers' hands?" Following the answer to this question Jesus stated, "Go and do the same" (Luke 10:36-37). If the context contains no such explanation of the meaning, the interpretation may be more difficult to determine.

Every parable has one central truth, one main lesson. There may be a number of subordinate teachings, but all the subordinate teachings will point to the central truth. Students should discover the central truth and let it guide their interpretation of the parable. Robert C. McQuilkin suggested three principles to observe in finding the central message:

1. Each parable has one, and only one, central message.

2. Each parable has a number of details that have a spiritual significance of their own, but all of these details relate to one central message.

3. Each parable has details that have no special spiritual significance.[25]

You must be careful not to "allegorize" a parable by attempting to draw from its small details spiritual teachings that are not obvious in the story itself and not in keeping with the purpose of the parable as revealed in the context. Stay with the main intent of the parable. The details in the story that have meaning are those reinforcing the central theme.

An interpretation of details in a parable must be guided by the storyteller Himself. Some of Christ's stories were clearly intended to illustrate several lessons. The parable of the prodigal son (Luke 15:11-32), for example, lays stress on the joy of the Father in forgiving His children, the nature of repentance, and the sin of jealousy and self-righteousness. We are safest if we stick to one main point in the application of a parable, making exceptions to this only in cases where Christ Himself treats His parable as an allegory by identifying several analogous details. In His parable of the tares and wheat (Matt. 13:24-30), for example, Jesus allegorized by identifying the sower as the Son of man, the field as the world, the good seed as the sons of the kingdom, the weeds as the sons of the devil, the enemy sower as the devil, the harvest as the close of the age, and the reapers as angels (Matt. 13:36-42).

Follow these guidelines in interpreting a parable:

- Study the setting (occasion) of the story.
- Get what light you can from the cultural background of the day.
- Read the story to get its natural meaning.
- Note the application made by the storyteller and the effect it had upon the hearers.
- Find the central teaching of the parable.
- Separate the more relevant details from the less significant ones.
- Check your interpretation with clear doctrine given elsewhere in the Scripture.
- Check your interpretation with reliable commentaries.
- Study the application of the parable's teaching to your own life and service.

The Allegory

You should understand the difference between a parable and an allegory. A *parable* is a short, descriptive story that illustrates a single truth or answers a single question. An *allegory* is a more elaborate story in which many, if not all, of the details have their counterparts in the application. The *Holman Bible Dictionary* says, "Allegory is a means of presenting or interpreting a story by focusing on hidden or symbolic meanings rather than the literal meaning."[26] *Parable* is derived from the Greek word *parabolē*, which means "putting things side by side." A similar, yet different, type of figurative language is the allegory, which by derivation means "saying things in a different way." Though a parable and an allegory are similar (A parable is a simile expanded, and an allegory is a metaphor expanded.), they have differences, as stated by J. R. McQuilkin:

> 1. A parable is realistic, but an allegory might not be. In an allegory, Christ might be a door or a vine, believers might be sheep or branches.
>
> 2. Though both might have a central theme, the parable is created to make one principal point, whereas the allegory might be created to teach many related or even unrelated truths.[27]
>
> 3. "Paul employed allegorical interpretations on four occasions (1 Cor. 5:6-8; 9:8-10; 10:1-11, Gal. 4:21-31—, once employing the word *allegory* itself (Gal. 4:24). Paul's allegories generally are restrained and focus on contemporary application."[28]

We should be careful not to allegorize the teachings of Scripture when it is not clear in the Scriptures themselves that our allegorization was intended by the Holy Spirit. Fanciful interpretations must be avoided, and the interpreter must be controlled by the context.

Try Key #12

A. Parable

To help you learn how to interpret a parable, read the parable of the lost sheep in Luke 15:1-7, and answer the questions below.

The *setting* of the parable (see vv. 1-3):

    1. What people, who were despised by religious Jews, were showing interest in Jesus' teaching? _____

  2. What people were grumbling about this? _____
  3. To whom did Jesus address the parable? _____
The *story* (see vv. 4-6):
  4. Of one hundred sheep, how many were lost? _____
  5. The shepherd went out to do what? _____
  6. What did he later ask his friends and neighbors to do?

  _____

The *spiritual application* (see v. 7):
  7. What is the central teaching of the parable? _____

  _____

  8. Who (from the "setting" above) are represented by the lost sheep or the "one sinner who repents"?
  9. Who (from the "setting" above) are represented by the "ninety-nine righteous persons who need no repentance"?

  _____

  10. Did Jesus mean (a) some people do not need to repent, or (b) some people are too self-righteous to see their need of repentance? _____

B. Allegory

Paul used an allegory of Abraham's two sons to drive home his teaching of justification through faith in Jesus Christ apart from the law. A number of analogies are drawn from the illustration. Look up the allegory in Galatians 4:21-31, and complete the following statements:
  1. Hagar and Sarah represent two different _____.
  2. Persons of two different spiritual conditions (bondage to the law and freedom in Christ) are represented by the _____ of these women.
  3. Bondage to the law is represented by the son of _____, the bondwoman.
  4. These mothers correspond to a present city and a future city, both named _____.
  5. Children of the promise are represented by the son named _____.

6. The believer is born through the promise, is free from the bondage of the law, and is born according to the _____.

Check your answers with the Answer List in the back of the book.

15.
Hebrew Poetry

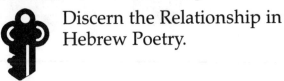 Discern the Relationship in
Hebrew Poetry.

> Roses are red, violets are blue,
> Sugar is sweet, and so are you.

This is poetry as we commonly know it in English. It has rhyme (the last word of the two lines rhyme) and rhythm (the pattern of flow is the same in the two lines).

Hebrew poetry is different. It has neither rhyme nor rhythm. The most common characteristic of Hebrew poetry is *parallelism*. Its style involves a rhythm of thought rather than a rhythm of sound. The thought of one line is related to the thought of another line. Take for example David's declaration in Psalm 34:1:

> I will bless the Lord at all times;
> His praise shall continually be in my mouth.

Basically, the thought is the same in both lines.

Varieties of Parallelism

Many varieties of parallelism appear in Hebrew poetry. You will be helped in your Bible study if you understand three basic kinds. Many of the other kinds are variations of these; but beware of trying to cram all forms of Hebrew poetry into these three. More extensive resources may be consulted for information on the other forms.[29] Parallelism is a fascinating characteristic of Hebrew poetry.

1. Synonymous Parallelism

When the thought of one line is repeated in different words

in another line, the parallelism is identified as *synonymous*. As you read Psalm 114, notice that every verse is a couplet of synonymous parallelism:

> When Israel went forth from Egypt,
> The house of Jacob from a people
>   of strange language,
>
> Judah became His sanctuary,
> Israel, His dominion.
>
> The sea looked and fled;
> The Jordan turned back.
>
> The mountains skipped like rams,
> The hills, like lambs.
>
> What ails you, O sea, that you flee?
> O Jordan, that you turn back?
>
> O mountains, that you skip like rams?
> O hills, like lambs?
>
> Tremble, O earth, before the Lord,
> Before the God of Jacob,
>
> Who turned the rock into a pool of water,
> The flint into a fountain of water.

2. Antithetic Parallelism

The opposite of synonymous parallelism is seen in *antithetic* parallelism. Instead of the thought of the first line being repeated in the second line, a contrasting idea is presented. The statement of the first line is affirmed, not by repetition, but by an opposite statement in the second line.

Antithetic parallelism is used oftentimes in the Proverbs, as in the following verses:

> The light of the righteous rejoices,
> But the lamp of the wicked goes out (13:9).

Fools mock at sin,
But among the upright there is
    good will (14:9).

Folly is joy to him who lacks sense,
But a man of understanding walks
    straight (15:21).

3. Synthetic Parallelism

When the thought is neither repeated nor contrasted but extended further, we have *synthetic* parallelism. Cause and effect are seen in the comparison of two lines. The second line adds a complementary thought to the first. The statement of the first line serves as the basis upon which the second one rests. The idea of the first line is given continuation in the second, and sometimes in the third and fourth lines.

Check out the synthetic parallelism in the following three verses:

And he will be like a tree firmly
    planted by streams of water,
Which yields its fruit in its season,
And its leaf does not wither;
And in whatever he does, he
    prospers (Ps. 1:3).

I lay down and slept;
I awoke, for the Lord sustains
    me (Ps. 3:5).

Yet those who wait for the Lord
Will gain new strength;
They will mount up with wings
    like eagles,
They will run and not get tired,
They will walk and not become
    weary (Isa. 40:31).

The category of "synthetic parallelism" in reality is not true parallelism. The second line does not balance the thought of the first. Instead, the thought is extended—it flows on. Notice this in Psalm 27:6a:

> And now my head will be lifted up
> above my enemies around me.

In synthetic parallelism the second line amplifies or complements the first, as in Psalm 55:6:

> And I say, "Oh, that I had wings like a dove!
> I would fly away and be at rest."

The three types of parallelism presented above have been recognized traditionally since they were defined by Robert Lowth of Oxford, England, around A.D. 1750. In 1988, Tremper Longman noted that the tendency of scholarship has been to increase the number of categories. Longman did not consider "synthetic" to be a helpful classification. He added four types to replace the synthetic but noted that they are "rough" guides to discovering the relationship between the two phrases of a poetic line.[30]

a. *Emblematic parallelism* explicitly draws an analogy, using a word of comparison (*like, as, so*) to bring together two thoughts from different spheres of life:

> As the deer pants for the water brooks,
> So my soul pants for Thee, O God (Ps. 42:1).

b. *Repetitive parallelism* begins with a statement in the first phrase that is partially repeated in the second but carried further:

> Ascribe to the Lord, O sons of the mighty,
> Ascribe to the Lord glory and strength.
> Ascribe to the Lord the glory due to His name;
> Worship the Lord in holy array (Ps. 29:1-2).

c. *Pivot pattern* includes in the middle of the poetic line a word or phrase that should be read with both the opening and closing phrases. For example, in Psalm 98:2 in the Hebrew, the phrase "to the nations" comes in the center and should be read with both the first and the last phrases. The intended meaning is that the Lord has made His salvation known to the nations, and has revealed His righteousness to the nations:

> The Lord has made His salvation known
>   to the nations
> and has revealed His righteousness (Ps. 98:2, Hebrew).

The NASB conveys the idea by translating the verse in this way:

> The Lord has made known His salvation;
>   He has revealed His righteousness
>   in the sight of the nations.

d. *Chiasm*, from the Greek letter *chi* that is formed by two crossing lines, identifies a parallelism in which the two center thoughts (one at the end of line 1 and the other at the beginning of line 2) are related, and the opening thought of line 1 and the closing thought of line 2 are related. Lines between the related thoughts would form an *X*:

> For   the Lord knows the way of the righteous,
> But   the way of the wicked will perish (Ps. 1:6).

Benefits of Parallelism

Parallelism in Hebrew poetry is a means of giving clear expression to the deep emotions of the writer. Since parallelism often means adding to the original thought, it contributes greatly to our understanding of the concepts that are conveyed by the writers. Parallelism reinforces meaning and increases clarity, and it helps to stick in the mind of the reader.

An understanding of Hebrew parallelism will aid you in interpreting poetical passages in the Bible. When you know that lines of Hebrew poetry are related and present similar, contrasting, or extended ideas, you will try to find the relationship. You will not take each thought in isolation but will seek to interpret it by its related idea within the passage.

See how this works with an example, Psalm 22:6:

> But I am a worm, and not a man,
> A reproach of men, and despised by the people.

Does the writer mean that he is humbling himself as a worm? Does he mean that he lacks self-esteem and considers himself to be without masculine dignity? We see that neither is the case when we relate the second line to the first. The speaker means that he is despised and rejected by his own people. Later he reveals that he finds relief and security in the Lord (vv. 24-31).

J. R. McQuilkin shared the following example of the way in which attention to parallelism can help in understanding the meaning of Scripture:

Fear is the chief word in the Old Testament describing a right relationship to God. But what does it mean to fear God? Many times Hebrew poetry helps in definitions of this kind. For example:

> If Thou, Lord, shouldst mark iniquities,
> O, Lord, who could stand?
> But there is forgiveness with thee,
> That Thou mayest be feared (Ps. 130:3-4).

As the psalmist adds the concept of "fear" to the idea of "forgiveness" a whole new dimension of meaning begins to come into focus. The loving, free forgiveness of God evokes a spirit of utter loyalty and awe-filled gratitude, not a craven shrinking from God in fearful anticipation of wrath.[31]

An added benefit of parallelism is discovered in the translating of Scripture from Hebrew into English or another language. The translator does not have to strive to find word translations that rhyme and phrases that fit into a meter.

Other Characteristics of Hebrew Poetry

There are a number of additional features of Hebrew poetry. Two will be mentioned here.

Stanzas or *strophes* usually are apparent in Hebrew poetry. A poem is divided into paragraphs on the basis of thought. Thought breaks give a poetic paragraphing and an increased clarity. A stanza usually consists of two, three, or four lines. Stanzas may be indicated by a constantly recurring refrain. Such divisions of larger sections of thought make it easier for the reader to grasp and to follow the flow of thought of the writer.

In some cases, poetry of the Old Testament is written in an *acrostic* or *alphabetical* form. The verses or sections begin with successive letters of the Hebrew alphabet. This may have served as a memory aid to the Hebrew reader, but it does not serve much purpose to the English reader except to indicate the beginning of verses or stanzas. The interval is one line in Psalm 111 and 112; two lines in Psalms 25, 34, 145; Proverbs 31:10-31; and Lamentations 4; three lines in Lamentations 1, 2, and 3; four lines in Psalms 9, 10, and 37; and sixteen lines in Psalm 119. Psalm 119 is the most famous of them. Check your Bible, and you will probably see that a Hebrew letter is recorded at the beginning of each stanza in Psalm 119.

Additional help for understanding poetry in the Psalms, including guidelines for interpreting special kinds of psalms, is offered by Mickelsen:

1. If possible, try to find the historical occasion for the particular psalm. The content of the psalm and the individual psalm title

often give clues. A good commentary may help. However, it is better to admit ignorance of the particular context than to assign it arbitrarily to a particular historical occasion if there is not enough evidence to justify such an assignment.

2. Try to understand the attitude, the outlook, the spiritual and psychological mood of the poet when he composed the psalm. Calvin called the Psalms, "an anatomy of all parts of the soul."

3. In dealing with the imprecatory psalms (those in which the psalmist hurls curses at his enemies) such as Psalm 109:6-20 and Psalm 137:7-9, regard such passages as poetic expressions of persons who were incensed at the tyranny of evil. . . .

4. In the messianic psalms (2, 16, 22, 40, 45, 69, 72, 98, 110 and others) note the elements that applied to the time of the writer as well as to the time of Christ. Consider why certain factors, because of what they involve, could only belong in the highest degree to the Messiah. The beauty of expression in these psalms must be appreciated in terms of the historical perspective at the time of their writing.

5. Observe the poet's basic convictions about God. The poet returns to these convictions when he feels the mounting pressures of life.[32]

Locations of Hebrew Poetry

The wisdom, or poetical, books of the Old Testament (Job, Psalms, Proverbs, Ecclesiastes, and Song of Solomon) all are written in Hebrew poetry. Much Hebrew poetry appears in the prophetical books also (Isaiah through Malachi). Some poetry is scattered through the other Old Testament books. Most modern translations (such as the RSV, NASB, and NIV) indicate Hebrew poetry by indentation and poetical form, as in the second of the first two verses of Isaiah 9:

But there will be no more gloom for her who was in anguish; in earlier times He treated the land of Zebulun and the land of Naphtali with contempt, but later on He shall make it glorious,

by the way of the sea, on the other side of Jordon, Galilee of the
Gentiles.

> The people who walk in darkness
> Will see a great light;
> Those who live in a dark land,
> The light will shine on them.

Did you notice the synonymous parallelism of the poetical
verse?

Try Key #13

Draw a line from each of the three words on the left below
to the appropriate definition on the right.

1. synonymous parallelism   a. contrasting idea presented
2. antithetic parallelism   b. similar idea expressed
3. synthetic parallelism   c. extended or additional idea

Psalm 37 includes all three types of Hebrew parallelism. Identify the type of parallelism that appears in each verse below
by putting in the blank the appropriate number from the list
above (1, 2, or 3):

_____ v. 2 For they will wither quickly like the grass,
           And fade like the green herb.

_____ v. 4 Delight yourself in the Lord;
           And He will give you the desires of your heart.

_____ v. 5 Commit your way to the Lord,
           Trust also in Him, and He will do it.

_____ v. 9 For evildoers will be cut off,
           But those who wait for the Lord,
               they will inherit the land.

_____ v. 13 The Lord laughs at him;
            For He sees his day is coming.

_____ v. 22 For those blessed by Him will inherit the land;
            But those cursed by Him will be cut off.

_____ v. 30 The mouth of the righteous utters wisdom;
            And his tongue speaks justice.

Check your answers with the Answer List in the back
of the book.

16.
Prophecy

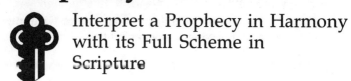 Interpret a Prophecy in Harmony
with its Full Scheme in
Scripture

Prophecy is a special revelation of God that predicts something in the future that is directly related to God's plan of
redemption. In its broadest sense, "prophecy" includes the
proclamation, or forthtelling, of truth as well as the prediction,
or foretelling, of the future. In this lesson we are using the term
in its strict sense of foretelling, that is, predictive prophecy.

Genesis 3:15, the *protevangelium* ("first gospel") is a prophecy of a continuing struggle between the descendants of
woman and the descendants of the serpent that ultimately
will end when the Messiah judges Satan. Genesis 12:2-3 is the
prophecy of divine blessing guaranteed to Abram that
through his seed, messianic blessings would come upon all
peoples of the earth.

Prophetic Principles

All the prophecies of Scripture blend together into one
harmonious scheme. Each individual prophecy must be
interpreted in the light of the complete prophetic program. In
declaring that "no prophecy of Scripture is a matter of one's
own interpretation" (2 Pet. 1:20), Peter affirmed that we cannot isolate one passage and interpret it apart from the entire
prophetic program. Passages related to a particular theme
must be harmonized. One prediction will shed light upon
another. Related to this basic principle are various other principles that are to be considered.

1. Figurative Language

Prophecy uses a great deal of figurative language. Watch for figures of speech, symbols, types, and Hebrew idioms in predictive prophecy. The first three of these have been covered elsewhere.

A Hebrew idiom is a style of expression contrary to the usual patterns of language or having a meaning different from the literal meaning. For example, the word *forever* is used in the Hebrew not only to mean "throughout endless ages" but sometimes to refer to the entire duration of a limited period of time. To become a person's servant "forever" meant till the end of life on earth (Deut. 15:17). The Passover Feast was to be celebrated as an "eternal" ordinance, that is, as long as the Jews were God's chosen channel on earth (Ex. 12:14). God's messianic kingdom will "endure forever," that is, until His purpose in a righteous earthly Kingdom is entirely fulfilled, and eternity is ushered in (Dan. 2:44).

Hendrichsen stated a principle for interpreting the language of prophecy:

> Interpret the words of the prophets in their usual, literal and historical sense, unless the context or manner in which they are fulfilled clearly indicates they have a symbolic meaning.[33]

2. Time Element

You should be aware that the time element is not strict in prophetic language. An experience that is future to the prophet's view may be spoken of as if it were *present* (Example: "For unto us a child is born, unto us a son is given," Isa. 9:6, KJV). A thing in the future may be spoken of as if it were *past* (Example: "But He was pierced through for our transgressions,/He was crushed for our iniquities," Isa. 53:5). The prophet, however, may refer to a future event in the *future* tense (Example: "All mankind will come to bow down before Me," Isa. 66:23).

3. Conditional Prophecies

Numerous times a condition is involved in a promise or warning of prophetic Scripture. A warning may be withdrawn if God in His mercy interposes between the threatening and the event. In such cases, the conditional nature of a prediction will be understood from a comparison of the prediction with the rest of Scripture, if it is not plainly stated in the passage itself.

An example of a conditional prediction is Jonah's warning to Nineveh that she would be destroyed in forty days (Jonah 3:4). When Nineveh repented, God withheld the judgment. A prophecy may depend on human agency and may, therefore, be conditional; but a prophecy that depends on God cannot be conditional unless conditions are clearly stated. You should, therefore, determine whether a prophecy is conditional or unconditional.

4. Double Fulfillment

A special feature that often appears in prophecy is double fulfillment. A prophecy that has a double fulfillment is one that relates to an immediate crisis but also to another event in the distant future.

Take for example Isaiah's prophecy, "Therefore the Lord Himself will give you a sign: Behold, a virgin will be with child and bear a son, and she will call His name Immanuel" (Isa. 7:14). The near fulfillment of this prophecy was the sign given to King Ahaz in the birth of a child to the prophetess who was a virgin at the time the prophecy was spoken, but later married Isaiah (Isa. 8:1-4). The far fulfillment was in the birth of Jesus through the Virgin Mary (Matt. 1:22-23).

Another double fulfillment is that of 2 Samuel 7:12-16, fulfilled first in Solomon and later in Christ (Heb. 1:5). Joel 2:28-32 is a third example, fulfilled first in the miracles of Pentecost (Acts 2:16-21) and, ultimately, at the time of Christ's second coming.

The reason God sometimes inspired widely separated events to be brought together in the scope of one prophecy is explained by Girdlestone as assuring the fulfillment of the latter by the fulfillment of the first:

> Yet another provision was made to confirm men's faith in utterances which had regard to the far future. It frequently happened that prophets who had to speak of such things were also commissioned to predict other things which would shortly come to pass; and the verification of these latter predictions in their own day and generation justified men in believing the other utterances which pointed to a more distant time. The one was practically a "sign" of the other, and if the one proved true the other might be trusted. Thus the birth of Isaac under the most unlikely circumstances would help Abraham to believe that in his seed all the families of the earth should be blessed.[34]

5. Twofold Perspective

Prophecy sometimes bears the special characteristic of twofold perspective. Sometimes the prophet would speak of two different events in the distant future as though they happened together when in reality they took place years apart.

The twofold perspective prophecies oftentimes relate to events of the first and second comings of Christ. The periods of our Lord's humiliation in His first coming and His glorification in His second coming are like two different mountain peaks viewed from afar by the Old Testament prophet and combined in prophecy as though they were to happen together.

Isaiah 61:1-3 is a clear example of the twofold perspective. Christ referred part of this prophecy to Himself when He read through "To proclaim the favorable year of the Lord" and stopped without reading "the day of vengeance of our God." He then declared, "Today this Scripture has been fulfilled in your hearing" (Luke 4:17-21). He applied to His first coming that part of the prophecy that referred to the year of grace, but He reserved the second part of the prophecy for a future period, the day of vengeance. Similar passages that contain twofold perspectives are Psalm 22 and Isaiah 9:6-7.

6. Central Themes

The central themes of prophecy are the Messiah's suffering and His triumph. Peter summed up the message of the prophets under these two headings: "the sufferings of Christ and the glories to follow" (1 Pet. 1:11). Christ did the same in His survey of Moses and the prophets for the two men on the road to Emmaus: "Was it not necessary for the Christ to suffer these things and to enter into His glory?" (Luke 24:26). The cross of Christ and the crown of Christ are the two focal points of Old Testament prophecy. Relate your study of prophecy to these two central themes. Prophecy should be interpreted Christologically because the Lord Jesus Christ is its central Person. John wrote, "The testimony of Jesus is the spirit of prophecy" (Rev. 19:10).

7. New Testament Reference

New Testament references to Old Testament prophecies are a key to understanding many prophecies. Check cross-references to discover such references. Sometimes the New Testament verse will interpret an Old Testament prophecy literally (Example: Christ's birthplace in Bethlehem, Mic. 5:2 and Matt. 2:6), sometimes figuratively (Example: Christ, the Shepherd who was smitten, Zech. 13:7 and Matt. 26:31), and sometimes spiritually (Example: Zion the spiritual abode of believers, Isa. 2:2-3 and Heb. 12:22). The relation of the two Testaments has been succinctly defined: "The Old is the New concealed, and the New is the Old revealed."

Sometimes a New Testament writer, under the inspiration of the Holy Spirit, interprets a prophecy in a way that we would not think to do. The Holy Spirit, who knows the correct interpretation of His Book, may do this, but we should be careful not to take such liberties. Henrichsen spoke to this point as follows:

> There will also be times when a New Testament writer will ascribe to an Old Testament passage a prophetic interpretation when the Old Testament passage does not appear to be pro-

phetic. You will find an example of this in Hosea. Israel had gone away from God and was referred to as the Lord's adulterous wife. God is speaking to Israel when He says, "When Israel was a youth I loved him, and out of Egypt I called My son" (Hosea 11:1). The original hearers could conclude, and rightly so, that this referred to Israel's deliverance from Egypt under Moses. But Matthew quotes this passage and says it is prophetic of Jesus Christ when Mary and Joseph returned with Him to Nazareth. "He was there [in Egypt] until the death of Herod, that what was spoken by the Lord through the prophet might be fulfilled, saying, 'Out of Egypt did I call My Son'" (Matthew 2:15).

We note that the Hosea passage is prophetic because Matthew, writing by inspiration of the Holy Spirit, says it is. In your Bible study you may not take such liberties. Matthew could because he wrote by inspiration of the Spirit, and the Spirit knew the correct interpretation of Hosea since He inspired that also. Matthew, however, does not tell you why he uses the prophecy from Hosea in that way.[35]

Try Key #14

Check out each of the above principles in a study of Genesis 3:15.

1. What figurative language is seen here? _____
2. Is the time element past, present, or future? _____
3. Is this a conditional prophecy? _____
4. Is there to be a double fulfillment of the prophecy? _____
5. Note a twofold perspective in this prophecy.
   a. Who is meant by "her seed" and "He"? _____
   b. When will the woman's seed be bruised on the heel? _____
   c. When will the serpent be bruised on the head? _____
6. Are both the central theme (first and second comings of Christ) referred to in the prophecy? _____

NOTE:
- Genesis 3:15 predicts a perpetual struggle between Satan's offspring and Eve's (Ps. 88:21, 22; 1 John 3:8-10, 13).
- Satan's seed are those serving his kingdom of darkness. Eve's seed is humanity at large and then Christ and those collectively in Him.
- Satan would cripple humankind, striking the heel; but Christ *the* seed would deliver the fatal blow, crushing Satan's head (Heb. 2:14-15; Rom. 16:20).
- Christ the Redeemer descended from Eve (Luke 3:23-38) and was made of a woman (Gal. 4:4-5), who also was a virgin (Isa. 7:14; Matt. 1:23). He was bone of our bone (Heb. 2:11, 14).
- Christ's heel was bruised when His feet were nailed to the cross; but ultimately, Christ will bruise Satan's head and overthrow him utterly (Rev. 12:9; 20:1-3,10; Col. 2:15).
- The effect of this victory is fortified by God's promise to His people (Ps. 19:13; Mark 16:18; Luke 10:18-19).

17.
Doctrinal Problems

 Examine the Full Teaching of Scripture on a Doctrine, Hold Complementary Truths in Balance, and Seek to Reconcile Alleged Problems.

You no doubt have heard someone say, "There are so many interpretations of the Bible, how can we know which one is correct?" or "There are so many contradictions in the Bible, how can we believe it?" These are questions often asked by persons who haven't studied the Bible much but who hold the suspicion that it cannot be understood and trusted.

In this lesson, let's consider how to establish a Scripture doctrine and how to deal with a paradox, a discrepancy, or any other problem faced in Bible study.

Doctrines

A doctrine is a teaching on a particular subject. The Christian faith is based upon the doctrines taught in Scripture. These were taught through life situations rather than in a systematic set of articles. Any truth of God, therefore, can be found in a number of places in the Bible. Hundreds of verses from various parts of the Bible may be relevant to a given doctrine.

Following are some guidelines for determining a Scriptural doctrine:

1. Compare Scripture Passages

Compare all the Scripture passages that relate to the particular subject rather than base a doctrine on one isolated passage. Study all that the Bible teaches on the subject. In formulating the doctrine, relate it to all biblical data that affects it.

2. Use Good Hermeneutics

Carefully employ the principles of hermeneutics in handling doctrinal passages. Do not disregard contextual and linguistic factors in interpreting a doctrine.

3. Use Clear Scriptural Passages

Base doctrine on plain and literal passages rather than on obscure, inferential, or figurative ones. Plain statements are needed for supporting doctrine.

4. Use Teaching Passages

Base doctrine on teaching passages rather than a historical passage. Teaching passages are doctrinal amplifications of historical passages. For example, the historical records of the Book of Acts are amplified and doctrinally crystallized in the New Testament Epistles, which are teaching passages. No doctrine should be based on Acts unless it is clearly taught in the Epistles.

5. Use a Balanced Approach

Do not overemphasize one aspect of truth to the detriment of another aspect of truth that is equally clear in Scripture. The doctrine of the sovereignty of God, for example, should not be emphasized to the point that human responsibility is disregarded. The Bible teaches both truths. We must emphasize what the Scripture emphasizes and avoid presenting one doctrine out of balance with another.

Paradoxes

There are some paradoxical truths in the Bible that we may not be able to fit together logically. When we find two truths in Scripture that we cannot perfectly reconcile, we must hold both truths in balance.

The doctrines oftentimes viewed as paradoxical are the

Trinity (How can God be one God and three Persons?), the dual nature of Christ (How can Jesus Christ be both God and man?), the origin and existence of evil (If evil did not coexist with God from eternity—and He did not create it— how did it come into existence?), and the sovereign election of God and the responsibility of human beings (Is salvation dependent upon God's sovereign election or human responsibility?).

Each of these sets of doctrine only appears to be contradictory to humanity's finite mind. We cannot comprehend the infinite mind of God. When the Bible teaches two doctrines that appear to be contradictory, we must follow its example and hold to both, keeping them in balance. Henrichsen also presented helpful advice regarding the handling of scriptural paradoxes:

> When the Bible leaves two conflicting doctrines unreconciled, so must you. Living in tension is not pleasant, but you must take care not to lose biblical balance in seeking to relieve the tension. Do not wrench the Scriptures apart in an attempt to force two conflicting doctrines into compromise.
>
> You can make application of such conflicting doctrines by preaching the right doctrine to the right person. For example, as a Christian you preach to yourself that God chose you; you did not choose Him. If the choice had been yours, you would have voted *against* Him. All you are and have is a gift of God's grace. This should fill you with humility and meekness.
>
> But you can boldly proclaim to the non-Christian that God loves him. For Jesus Himself said, "God so loved the *world*, that He gave His only begotten Son" (John 3:16).[36]

Apparent Discrepancies (Alleged Problems)

There are in Scripture what may appear to be discrepancies. Because the Bible is God-breathed and inerrant, the discrepancies are only apparent. Any real contradiction or error will not be found. We can discover a possible solution for any apparent problem in the Bible, and we are not obligated to solve every problem. Robertson McQuilkin explained the Christian's handling of apparent discrepancies in Scripture:

> Because our presupposition is that the Bible is true in all its parts, we seek solutions when there appears to be error. When we cannot solve a problem, we admit it. We do not conclude, however, that it cannot be solved. Rather, because of loyalty built on the solid foundation of strong evidence of trustworthiness, and honestly facing the alternatives with which disloyalty would leave us, we hold in abeyance problems yet unsolved. We do not grant that a problem is unsolvable and then proceed to interpret the passage as if it were in error. Furthermore, we hold that a *possible* solution is all that is demanded. We do not have to prove that a possible interpretation is *the* correct solution, but simply that there is a reasonable solution to the apparent problem. Since the Bible has proved itself trustworthy through the ages, we hold it innocent until proved guilty. The accuser must prove error. When problems are unresolved, it is not the Bible that is wrong, but rather our understanding of it. We wait either for more evidence or for a better theory to more coherently explain the evidence.[37]

Some writers such as Edward J. Young and Harold Lindsell have dealt with apparent contradictions of the Bible and have presented reasonable explanations of the passages. Oftentimes a critical commentary also will present insight concerning alleged problems in the passage under study. When dealing with a Bible problem, you should consult such tools for help.

In his dealing with discrepancies in Scripture, Harold Lindsell charged that the real difficulty is a want of biblical faith rather than a want of evidence:

> I do not wish with a casual wave of my hand to dismiss the questions that critics have raised about errors in Scriptures.

However, I do not think the problem areas constitute a threat to biblical infallibility nor do I think that there are insoluble difficulties. This does not mean that I can provide a ready solution to every datum raised by those who oppose inerrancy. I can say, however, that a multitude of what formerly were difficulties have been solved, so that the detractors have had to back water again and again. But as each apparent discrepancy is resolved, another objection is raised. Although in hundreds of cases criticisms of Scripture have been shown to be unfounded, those who refuse to believe in inerrancy never seem to be satisfied.[38]

Condoning of Evil

Did God condone a lot of murder in the Old Testament after He commanded "You shall not murder" (Ex. 20:13)? Did He condone the polygamy of David and Solomon after commanding that a king of Israel should never "multiply wives for himself" (Deut. 17:17)? And did God overlook slavery in spite of the equality of all people before their Creator God?

These are questions that face one who makes a serious study of God's Word. A study of the full revelation of Scripture reveals that God never condones murder, but He does sanction human governments as His own "ministers" for the punishment of evil (Rom. 13:1-7; 1 Tim. 2:2; Titus 3:1). McQuilkin said this concerning the questions of polygamy and slavery in Bible times:

> The teaching of Scripture must be judged in light of the times. Revelation was progressive or cumulative, and God always deals with people as and where they are.

> For example, though neither polygamy nor slavery are approved or promoted in Scripture, both are recognized and dealt with in Scripture in terms of the conditions of society. God's eternal principles of mercy and justice were infused into these basically unjust and unmerciful structures until people came to the place where the structure itself could be changed. Christ Himself referred to this phenomenon when He said of divorce

that from the beginning it was not God's will, but Moses permitted it because of their hardness of heart (Mark 10:6)[39]

Quotations

There are in the New Testament nearly three hundred quotations from the Old Testament. The careful Bible student will confront questions concerning these quotations. He will find that an Old Testament passage in his Bible may be quite different from the way it is quoted in the New Testament.

Mickelsen suggested the following guidelines for understanding Old Testament quotations in the New Testament:

1. Remember that New Testament writers were quoting from memory, usually *without* the Old Testament scrolls in front of them. Do not expect word for word exactness.

2. Most of the quotations are from the Septuagint, the Greek translation of the Old Testament made about 250 to 150 B.C. By the very nature of translations, we cannot expect the Septuagint translators to give exactly the same translations as our twentieth-century translators, especially since the Hebrew text was written without vowels.

3. The New Testament writers used quotations the way other writers of their day used quotations—not with the exact preciseness demanded by twentieth-century technology. They also adapted them for their purposes.

4. The New Testament writers recognized the authority of the Old Testament—that it was God's Word. That is why they quoted it so frequently.[40]

In addition to these guidelines, we should note that God Himself is the Author of both the Old Testament and the New Testament; and as the Author, God has the right to reword any quotation to more clearly interpret His intended meaning for the reader.

Try Key #15

I hope that you now feel more comfortable about facing Bible problems. Let's see how you handle this Bible problem: Was God responsible for David's taking of a census, or was Satan responsible? Bible critics have claimed that a contradiction is found in the two parallel accounts:

Now again the anger of the Lord burned against Israel, and it incited David against them to say, "Go, number Israel and Judah" (2 Sam. 24:1)

Then Satan stood up against Israel and moved David to number Israel (1 Chron. 21:1).

1. Do you believe that the two statements are to be viewed as (a) contradictory, or (b) complementary? _____
2. What light does each of the following passages shed upon the question?
    (a) James 1:13: _____
    (b) Job 1:9-12; 2:4-6: _____
    (c) 2 Corinthians 12:7-9: _____
_____

3. How would you explain the seeming contradiction of the two verses in 2 Samuel and 1 Chronicles? _____
_____

Check your answers with the Answer List in the back of the book.

Notes

1. A. Berkeley Mickelsen, *Interpreting the Bible* (Grand Rapids, Wm. B. Eerdmans Publishing Co., 1977), 20-21.

2. A. C. Blackman, *Biblical Interpretation* (Philadelphia: The Westminster Press, 1957), 112.

3. Kenneth Hagen, et. al., *The Bible in the Churches* (New York: Paulist Press, 1985), 5.

4. Ibid., 102-103.

5. Bernard Ramm, *Protestant Biblical Interpretation* (Grand Rapids: Baker Book House, 1970), 90.

6. Walter A. Henrichsen, *Understand* (Colorado Springs, Colo.: NavPress, 1977), 59-60.

7. Robertson McQuilkin, *Understanding and Applying the Bible* (Chicago: Moody Press, 1983), 109-110.

8. Mickelsen, *Interpreting the Bible*, 112.

9. McQuilkin, *Understanding and Applying the Bible*, 175.

10. Ibid., 179-180.

11. Ibid.

12. T. Norton Sterrett, *How to Understand Your Bible* (Downers Grove, Ill.: Inter-Varsity Press, 1974), 86.

13. Mickelsen, *Interpreting the Bible*, 178.

14. Porter G. Perrin and George H. Smith, *The Perrin-Smith Handbook of Current English* (Chicago: Scott, Foresman and Co., 1955), 289.

15. Irving L. Jensen, *Independent Bible Study* (Chicago: Moody Press, 1963), 67-68.

16. *Webster's New World Dictionary of the American Language* (New York: The World Publishing Co., 1970), n.p.

17. *Webster's New World Dictionary,* n.p.

18. Mickelsen, *Interpreting the Bible*, 278-279.

19. A Berkeley Mickelsen and Alvera M. Mickelsen, *Better Bible Study* (Glendale, Calif.: G/L Publications, 1977), 144-145.

20. Sterrett, *How to Understand Your Bible*, 114.

21. McQuilkin, *Understanding and Applying the Bible*, 226.

22. Robert C. McQuilkin, *Our Lord's Parables* (1929; reprint, Grand Rapids: Zondervan Publishing House, 1980), 17.

23. Ibid., 21.

24. The Mickelsens, *Better Bible Study*, 131-132.

25. R. McQuilkin, *Our Lord's Parables*, 22.

26. Trent C. Butler, gen. ed., "Allegory," in *Holman Bible Dictionary* (Nashville: Holman Bible Publishers, 1991), 35.

27. McQuilkin, *Understanding and Applying the Bible*, 159.

28. Butler, *Holman Bible Dictionary*, 35.

29. See Andrew E. Hill and John H. Walton, *A Survey of the Old Testament* (Grand Rapids: Zondervan Publishing House, 1991), 247-262; William Sanford LaSov, David Allan Hubbard, and Frederic Wm. Bush, *Old Testament Survey: The Message, Form, and Background of the Old Testament* (Grand Rapids: Eerdmans, 1982), 307-318.

30. Tremper Longman, *How to Read the Psalms* (Downers Grove, Ill.: Inter-Varsity Press, 1988), 89-100.

31. McQuilkin, unpublished document.

32. The Mickelsens, *Better Bible Study*, 121-122.

33. Henrichsen, *Understand*, 76.

34. R. B. Girdlestone, *The Grammar of Prophecy* (London: Eyre and Spottiswoode, 1901), 21.

35. Henrichsen, *Understand*, 77-78.

36. Ibid., 99.

37. McQuilkin, *Understanding and Applying the Bible*, 204.

38. Harold Lindsell, *The Battle for the Bible* (Grand Rapids: Zondervan Publishing House, 1976), 161.

39. McQuilkin, unpublished document.

40. The Mickelsens, *Better Bible Study*, 167.

Books to Use as Tools for Interpretation

As we are indebted to our forefathers for their inventions of tools that enable us to fulfill the responsibilities of life with greater facility, we owe much to students of the Scriptures who have published "tools" that we may use in Bible study and interpretation. Following is a list of helpful tools with suggestions of use. A careful reading and study of the Scripture itself, with prayerful dependence upon the Holy Spirit for illumination, is the first step necessary in Bible interpretation. Beyond this initial step, these tools may be helpful.

Hermeneutics

Some of the most helpful books that cover the broad field of hermeneutics and give principles for biblical interpretation are the following:

Berkhof, Louis. *Principles of Biblical Interpretation.* Grand Rapids: Baker Book House, 1950.

Dockery, David S. and Clendenen, Ray, eds. *The New American Commentary.* Nashville: Broadman Press, 1991.

McQuilkin, Robertson. *Understanding and Applying the Bible.* Chicago: Moody Press, 1983.

Mickelsen, A. Berkeley. *Interpreting the Bible.* Grand Rapids: Wm. B. Eerdmans Publishing Co., 1963.

Ramm, Bernard. *Protestant Biblical Interpretation*. Boston: W. A. Wilde Co., 1956.

Sproul, R. C. *Knowing Scripture*. Downers Grove, Ill.: Inter-Varsity Press, 1982.

Terry, Milton S. *Bible Hermeneutics*. Grand Rapids: Zondervan Publishing House, n.d.

You may refer to one or more of these tools to gain a grasp of the general rules to follow in interpreting the Bible. They cover both general and special hermeneutics and the particular types of "keys" under each.

Grammatical Analysis
(Literal interpretation, author's intention, grammar, and context)

Two tools helpful in grammatical analysis in Bible study are suggested:

Jensen, Irving L. *Independent Bible Study*. Chicago: Moody Press, 1963.

Traina, Robert A. *Methodical Bible Study*. Wilmore, Ky.: Robert A. Traina, 1952.

These tools aid in analyzing a Bible book or passage to determine the meaning the author intended to convey. Read and apply the lessons these books present for technical assistance in inductive Bible study.

Bible commentaries are additional tools for acquiring the meaning of a passage. Consult especially those commentaries that explain the meanings of the original language. Compare commentaries to get a balanced, accurate view of the passage.

Greek and Hebrew study tools are helpful in grammatical analysis for students who have an introduction to the original languages.

Background
(Historical setting, purpose and plan)

Tools helpful in understanding the setting and objective of a book or passage are the Bible handbook, Bible encyclopedia or dictionary, Bible introduction, and Bible atlas. One of each is suggested here (including both an Old Testament and a New Testament introduction):

Alexander, David and Pat, eds. *Eerdman's Handbook to the Bible.* Grand Rapids: William B. Eerdmans Publishing Co., 1973.

Archer, Gleason L., ed. *A Survey of Old Testament Introduction.* Chicago: Moody Press, 1974.

Beitzel, Barry J., *The Moody Atlas of Bible Lands.* Chicago: Moody Press, 1985.

Butler, Trent C., gen. ed. *Holman Bible Dictionary.* Nashville: Holman Bible Publishers, 1991.

Dockery, David S., ed., *Holman Bible Handbook.* Nashville: Holman Bible Publishers, 1992.

Douglas, J. D., ed., *The New Bible Dictionary.* Grand Rapids: William B. Eerdmans Publishing Co., 1962.

Guthrie, Donald. *New Testament Introduction.* Downers Grove, Ill.: Inter-Varsity Press, 1970.

Tenney, Merrill C., ed. *Zondervan Pictorial Encyclopedia of the Bible.* Grand Rapids: William B. Eerdmans Publishing Co., 1975.

Look up the title of the Bible book (and in some cases its geographical location) in either of these tools in your search for background information such as origin, destination, occasion, purpose and plan, characters, chronology, and historical-geographical background. In the dictionary or encyclopedia, you may look up the name of the author of the Bible book, as well as the title of the book and its geographical location.

Word Use
(Word Meaning, related Scripture, figures of speech)

The Bible dictionary and the Bible encyclopedia are helpful as a first reference for discovering word meanings. Other helpful tools are the following:

Bullinger, E. W. *Figures of Speech Used in the Bible*. Grand Rapids: Baker Book House, 1968.

Canne, et al. *The Treasury of Scripture Knowledge*. McLean, Va.: MacDonald Publishing Co., 1982.

Girdlestone, R. B. *Synonyms of the Old Testament*. Grand Rapids: William B. Eerdmans Publishing Co., 1953.

Nave, Orville J. *The New Nave's Topical Bible*. Grand Rapids: Zondervan Publishing House, 1969.

Strong, James. *Strong's Exhaustive Concordance of the Bible*. Nashville: Holman Bible Publishers, n.d.

Vine, W. E. *The Expanded Vine's Expository Dictionary of New Testament Words*. Minneapolis, Minn.: Bethany House Publishers, 1984.

Girdlestone's and Vine's word-study books provide definitions of words used in Scripture along with meanings in the original languages, biblical usages, and references to Bible passages where the words are used.

The concordance directs the student to Scripture verses that use a particular word. *Nave's Topical Bible* brings together verses that are related to a general topic. *The Treasury of Scripture Knowledge* directs you to numerous biblical references related subject-wise to a particular reference that you turn to in its biblical order.

Bullinger's book deals with figures of speech per se.

Use these tools to determine the meaning of particular words you encounter in your Bible study as well as the usage of the words elsewhere in Scripture.

Special Hermeneutics

Special hermeneutics deal with forms of material and special themes that occur in the Bible. To guide you in the application of the principles that help you to understand these special types of language, the following tools are suggested. These deal with parables, poetry, problems in Scripture, and prophetical language (biblical prophecy, symbols, and types):

Archer, Gleason L., Jr. *Encyclopedia of Bible Difficulties.* Grand Rapids: Zondervan Publishing House, 1982.

Biederwolf, William E. *The Second Coming Bible.* Reprint. Grand Rapids: Baker Book House, 1982.

Holman Topical Concordance: An Index to the Bible Arranged by Subjects in Alphabetical Order. Nashville: Holman Bible Publishers, 1973.

Kissinger, Warren S. *The Parables of Jesus: A History of Interpretation and Bibliography.* Metuchen, N.J.: Scarecrow Press, Inc., 1979.

Ludwigson, Raymond. *A Survey of Bible Prophecy.* Grand Rapids: Zondervan Publishing House, 1973.

Yoder, Sanford C. *Poetry of the Old Testament.* Scottdale, Pa.: Herald Press, 1948.

Appendix:
Bible Marking

Advantages of Bible Marking

Highlights truths to be emphasized. Disciplines you to look for important points and helps you to retain good ideas.

Suggestions

Avoid illegible markings (use a rule, a good pen, and good penmanship). Avoid indiscriminate marking (use appropriate marks for appropriate items). Work out your own system, then stick with it. Some ideas follow you may want to adopt as your own.

A. Line Marks (in order of emphasis)
   1. Underlining (keys words, not long sections)
   2. Wavy underline (greater emphasis than straight)
   3. Connecting lines ("rail-road" between related words in different sections)
   4. Brackets (bracket symbols to section in key phrases or verses)
   5. Marginal line (vertical line in margin beside important passage)
   6. Double/triple marginal line (stronger emphasis than single vertical line)
   7. Box (four-side box to box in a very special verse or paragraph)

B. *Printing*
   1. Overwriting (bold print superimposed over key words)
   2. Numbering or lettering (to note *lists* of ideas—over words or in the margin)

OUR FAMILY PSALM

Psalm 34 (N.I.V.)

Of David. When he pretended to be insane
before Abimelech, who drove him away, and
he left. (I Sam. 21)

A1
B5   *A fixed resolution* ⟨

¹I will extol the LORD at all times;
  his praise will always be on my lips.
²My soul will boast in the LORD;
  let the afflicted hear and rejoice.

A4
B1

[³Glorify the LORD with me;
  let us exalt his name together.]

⁴I sought the LORD, and he answered me;
  he delivered me from all my fears.

A2
A6

⁵Those who look to him are radiant;
  their faces are never covered with
    shame.
⁶This poor man called, and the LORD heard
    him;
  he saved him out of all his troubles.

A5

⁷The angel of the LORD encamps around
    those who fear him,
  and he delivers them. (1970 trip)

A3

⁸Taste and see that the LORD is good;
  blessed is the man who takes refuge in
    him.
⁹Fear the LORD, you his saints,
  for those who fear him lack nothing.

B5

¹⁰The lions may grow weak and hungry, *Lions/believers*
  but those who seek the LORD lack no
    good thing. (1954 - - -)

D1, B1

✡ ¹¹Come, my children, listen to me;
  I will teach you the fear of the LORD.

B6

David determined to serve God (v. 1-2), & calls
others to do so (v. 3). Good reasons: His Name,
salvation, provision, protection, peace.

V. 1-10 – Praise to God
V. 11-22- Address to men

12 Whoever of you loves life
  1 and desires to see many good days,
13 keep your <u>tongue from evil</u>   B2
  2 and your lips from speaking lies. - guile,
14 Turn from evil and do good;   dishonesty   > B5
  3 seek <u>peace</u> and pursue it. / 1 Pet. 3:10-11

15 The <u>eyes of the Lord</u> are on the righteous   A3
  and his <u>ears are</u> attentive to their cry;
16 the <u>face of the</u> Lord is against those who
      do evil,
  to cut off the memory of them from the
    earth.

17 The righteous <u>cry out</u>, and <u>the Lord hears</u> | A5
    them;
  he delivers them from all their troubles.

18 The Lord is close to the brokenhearted   A7
  and saves those who are crushed in
      spirit.   No trouble is

19 A righteous man may have many   so great
    troubles,   that He B5
  but the <u>Lord delivers him</u> from them all; cannot !
                                      deliver!

20 he protects all his bones,
  not one of them will be broken.

21 Evil will slay the wicked;
    the foes of the righteous will be
      condemned.
22 The Lord redeems his servants;
    no one will be condemned who <u>takes</u>
          <u>refuge</u> in him.

    We have all the providential help   B5
    we need.

      3. Printing in various type sizes (larger for emphasis)
      4. Top notes: major headings and outlines
      5. Side margin notes: incidental notes
      6. Bottom notes: important ideas derived from study

Additional ideas for Bible marking—not used as widely as the above—are as follows:

  C. Highlighter (Light-shaded felt tip that covers the words to highlight them) This may be used in addition to or in place of items under "A" and/or "B1" above.

  D. Symbols
      1. Star - by excellent point or special promise
      2. Letter codes: P - promise, C - challenge, K - key to the church, etc.
      3. Exclamation mark - by commands of God to us
      4. Question mark - by problem verses or ideas (to be investigated)
      5. Drawings: stick figure, cloud, crown, cross, arrow

  E. Colors
    The following color scheme may be used for underlining:
      1. Red - salvation (blood)
      2. Green - Christian life (growth)
      3. Blue - God, Person and attributes (sky)
      4. Purple - special blessing (royalty, from Him)
      5. Yellow - prophecy (light of the future)
      6. Brown - sin and judgment (decay, ruin)

Answer List

Chapter 1

Needs for the Bible student: 1. Desire; 2. Dependence; 3. Discipline
A. 1. Christ; 2. Soul; 3. God; 4. Life.
B. 1. Mirror (conviction); 2. Fire and hammer (breaking); 3. Water (cleansing); 4. Food (strength and growth); 5. Light (guidance); 6. Sword (victory); 7. Money (spiritual success); 8. Seed (fruitful ministry).

Chapter 3

1-B; 2-A.

Chapter 4

B.

Chapter 5

Christ is able to turn adversity into blessing, to send help in time of great need, to teach His power through fellowship in His sufferings, and to teach contentment in any situation.

Chapter 6

Are your answers similar to these?
Theme: Joy in Suffering. I. Paul's Thanksgiving and Prayer for the Philippian Christians; II. Paul's Present Circumstances; III. Exhorta-

tion to Live Worthy of the Gospel; IV. Plan to Send Helpers to Philippi; V. Warning Against Lapse; VI. Exhortation and Appreciation.

Chapter 7

1. a.—every moment throughout time, b.—each time they are remembered; 2. the soul departed from the body and present with the Lord; 3. No, maturing but not sinless.

Chapter 8

1. In absolutely *nothing* be anxious; 2. The plural *you* refers to all the saints in the church, (b).

Chapter 9

Physical body, present existence.

Chapter 10

A. Israel; B. Yes; C. No; D. They required all uncircumcised Christians to be circumcised as a necessary part of salvation; E. A Jew who did not accept Jesus Christ as the Messiah was not a true believer; neither was one who added works to faith as necessary for salvation. Though one was changed outwardly by physical circumcision, one's heart was not changed; he, therefore, did not truly belong to God.

Chapter 11

1-B; 2-A; 3-E; 4-C; 5-D; 6. simile; 7. personification; 8. apostrophe; 9. synecdoche; 10. metaphor.

Chapter 12

1. Flaming sword; 2. burning bush; 3. blood; 4. baskets of figs; 5. wheels; 6. seals.

Chapter 13

1. "Priest according to the order of Melchizedek"; 2. perpetual, permanent priest; He lives forever as our Priest; 3. all except e. and g.

Chapter 14

A. 1. Tax-gatherers, sinners; 2. Pharisees, scribes; 3. the grumblers; 4. one; 5. find the lost sheep; 6. "Rejoice"; 7. heaven rejoices over a sinner's repentance; 8. tax collectors, sinners; 9. Pharisees, scribes; 10. b.
B. 1. covenants (v. 24); 2. sons (vv. 22-23); 3. Hagar (vv. 24-25); 4. Jerusalem (vv. 25-26); 5. Isaac (v. 28); 6. Spirit (v. 29).

Chapter 15

1. b.; 2. a; 3. c.; v. 2-1; v. 4-3; v.5-3; v. 9-2; v. 13-3; v. 22-2; v. 30-1.

Chapter 16

1. Seed, bruise head, bruise heel; 2. future; 3. no; 4. no; 5. a. Christ; 5. b. the cross; 5. c. final defeat of Satan; 6. yes.

Chapter 17

1. (b); 2 (a); God does not tempt; 2 (b) He allows Satan to tempt; 2 (c) When He does, God has a purpose for good; 3. God found sin in Israel, and He used David's transgression in the census as an occasion to chastise Israel. God permitted Satan to tempt David, and David yielded to the temptation. David was not forced to succumb to Satan's temptation, but he did. God's judgment that already had threatened David and his kingdom was proven to be necessary by the test.